340 Christian & Inspirational

PATTERNS FOR SCROLL SAW WOODWORKERS

THIRD EDITION
Revised & Expanded

Ascension,
Pattern on page 122

340 Christian & Inspirational

PATTERNS FOR SCROLL SAW WOODWORKERS

THIRD EDITION
Revised & Expanded

BY TOM L. ZIEG

FOX CHAPEL
PUBLISHING

Author Dedication
This book is dedicated to those who played a role in my Christian upbringing.

ISBN: 978-1-4971-0487-7

The Cataloging-in-Publication Data is on file with the Library of Congress.

Managing Editor: Gretchen Bacon
Acquisitions Editor: Kaylee J. Schofield
Editor: Joseph Borden
Designer: Matthew Hartsock
Proofreader: Kelly Umenhofer
Indexer: Camille Morrison

To learn more about the other great books from Fox Chapel Publishing, or to find a retailer near you, call toll-free 800-457-9112, send mail to 903 Square Street, Mount Joy, PA 17552, or visit us at *www.FoxChapelPublishing.com.*

We are always looking for talented authors. To submit an idea, please send a brief inquiry to acquisitions@foxchapelpublishing.com.

Printed in China
First printing

Contents

Introduction

Using a scroll saw can be a very satisfying and stimulating form of relaxation. With a scroll saw, a woodworker can turn scrap wood into beautiful gifts and useful household items.

Some of the projects can be completed with just the scroll saw. Most of the projects will require the use of a hand or electric drill. However, a selection of easy projects is included to help the beginner succeed while increasing his/her confidence and ability. Many medium to complex patterns intended for the more experienced scroll sawer are also included.

This book is simply about ideas. An endeavor has been made to present a series of designs along with their symbolism to enable the reader to understand how the designs were derived. I hope that the beginner and experienced scroller alike will find something of interest herein.

The woodworker should not feel confined to using the patterns exactly as illustrated. The patterns may be changed to meet specific needs by reducing or enlarging.

Cutting out many of the patterns in this book produces very delicate or fragile parts. A very fine blade is a necessity. The woodworker must have good control and cut carefully and slowly.

To cut the patterns in this book, I used a 16" (40.6cm), two-speed scroll saw. The slower speed setting provides the control needed to make the intricate cuts required by the patterns. Using the slower speed extends the time necessary to complete the project, but also ensures the project will turn out nicely.

I used an assortment of different blades in my scroll saw. I made the intricate lettering cuts with a very fine-tooth blade (27 teeth per inch). Although the blade is designed for cutting thicknesses up to ³⁄₃₂" (2.4mm), the slow speed allows much thicker wood to be cut.

Usually, you should make the interior cuts of the patterns first. Work from the center of the pattern outward to avoid putting pressure on the areas already cut. Each smaller element of the pattern should be cut from the inside out, just like the overall larger pattern. This method of cutting becomes particularly important for lettering. See the example below.

If the outside of the letter was cut first, the saw pressure and vibration could break the appendage off at the narrow connecting bridge. Cutting the outside last will give the appendage the support needed.

I hope this book brings you much pleasure and enjoyment as you learn from each design and make your own woodworking heirlooms.

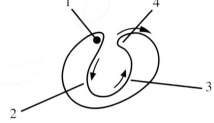

Cut in the direction of 1-4

Christmas Candle Appliqué
page 129

What You Can Make Using This Book

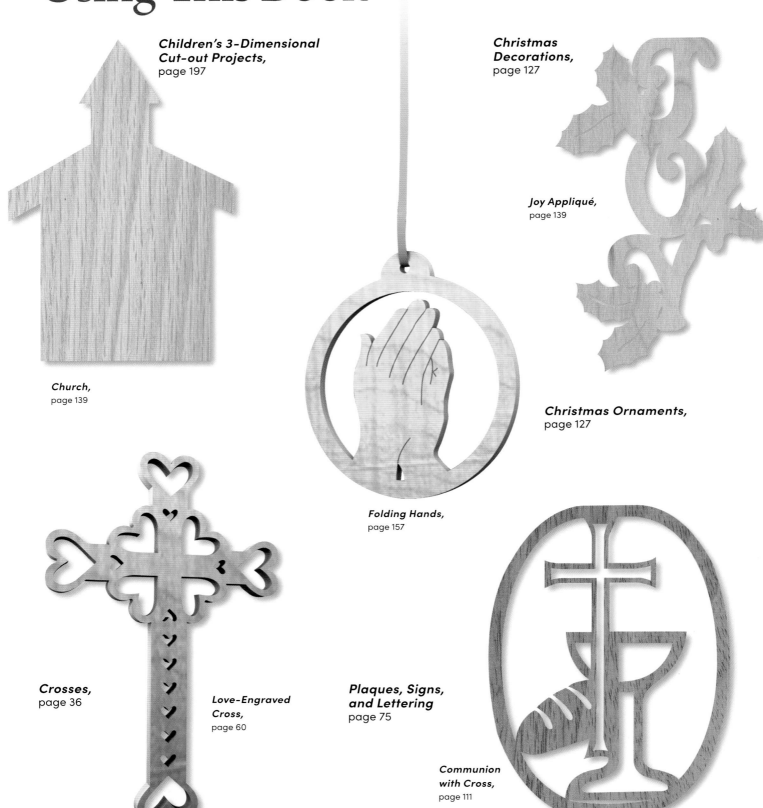

Children's 3-Dimensional Cut-out Projects,
page 197

Christmas Decorations,
page 127

Joy Appliqué,
page 139

Church,
page 139

Christmas Ornaments,
page 127

Folding Hands,
page 157

Crosses,
page 36

Love-Engraved Cross,
page 60

Plaques, Signs, and Lettering
page 75

Communion with Cross,
page 111

Jigsaw Puzzle Ornaments,
page 187

Angel,
page 187

IHS,
page 216

Letters and Words,
page 216

Letter Openers,
page 195

Chi Rho,
page 195

Plaques, Signs, and Lettering
page 75

Puzzles,
page 209

Dove Peace Appliqué,,
page 88

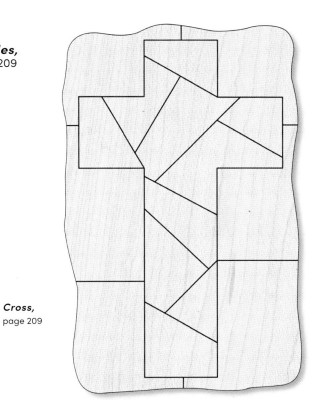

Cross,
page 209

Jesus in Prayer, fretwork portrait, by Santomarco Enzo (Italy). Pattern on page 125

Gallery

The following pages are chock-full of Christian-inspired scroll saw art, pulled from the archives of the first and second editions and the pages of *Scroll Saw Woodworking & Crafts* magazine. These inspiring pieces of art—fretwork, intarsia, portraits, ornaments, and more—will motivate you to expand on the patterns in this book and design your own creations.

Floral Fretwork Cross,
by Tim Andrews.
Pattern on page 37

In His Arms,
segmentation plaque, by
Robin Balls.
Pattern on page 126

Nativity Scene,
traditional German lichterbogen
(lighted arch), by Tom Sevy and
Volker Arnold.

Pattern on page 103

Pattern on page 146–147

Pattern on page 37

Pattern on page 131

Pattern on page 36

Star, Pattern on page 158

Bethlehem Star, Pattern on page 159

Patterns on page 170

Pattern on page 105

Pattern on page 105

Pattern on page 111

Chi Rho,
Pattern on page 219

Mission Cross,
Pattern on page 48

Crucifix Pattern,
on page 63

Church,
Pattern on page 197

Candle,
Pattern on page 148

Children Praying,
Patterns on page 203

Jesus Saves Plaque,
Pattern on page 91

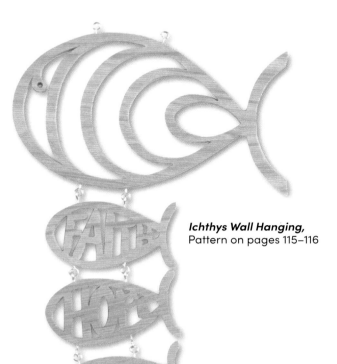

Ichthys Wall Hanging,
Pattern on pages 115–116

Ascension,
Pattern on page 122

Daily Bread Trivet,
Pattern on page 103

Various Crosses

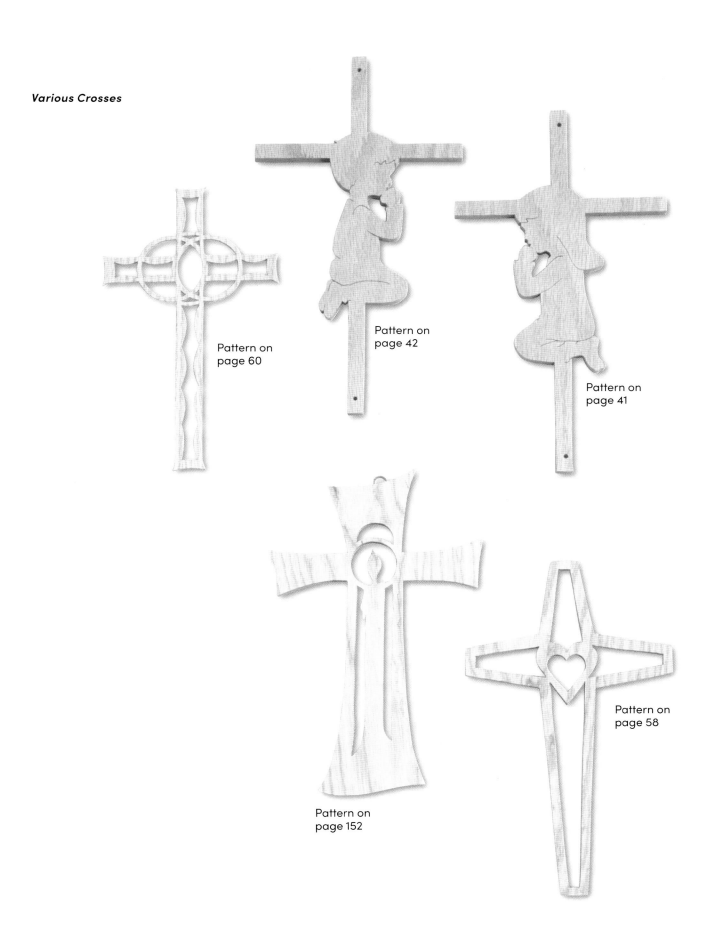

Pattern on
page 60

Pattern on
page 42

Pattern on
page 41

Pattern on
page 152

Pattern on
page 58

Pattern on page 105

Pattern on page 114

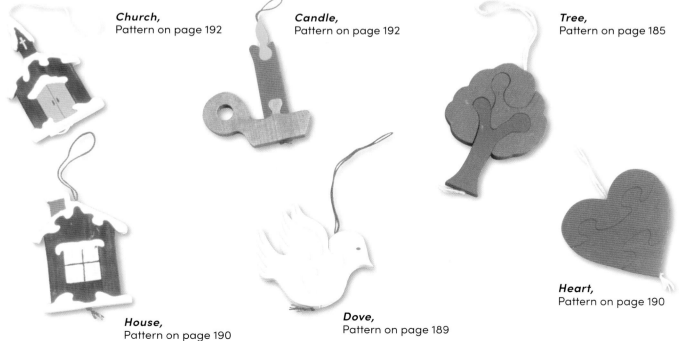

Church,
Pattern on page 192

Candle,
Pattern on page 192

Tree,
Pattern on page 185

House,
Pattern on page 190

Dove,
Pattern on page 189

Heart,
Pattern on page 190

Butterfly,
Pattern on page 192

Fish,
Pattern on page 189

Star,
Pattern on page 191

Apple,
Pattern on page 185

Wreath,
Pattern on page 191

Bell,
Pattern on page 191

Chistmas Tree Mail Holder,
Pattern on page 131

Dove Mail Holder,
Pattern on page 37

Cross Mail Holder,
Pattern on page 36

Symbol of Faith,
Victorian cross,
by John A. Nelson and Ben Fink.
Pattern on page 74

Intarsia Nativity Set,
Intarsia ornaments, by Kathy Wise.

Star of Bethlehem,
3-D Victorian fretwork ornament.
Pattern on pages 70–71

Holiday Silhouettes,
fretwork ornaments,
by Tom Zieg.

The Last Supper
fretwork plaque, by Tom Zieg.
Pattern on page 125

Christmas Greetings,
fretwork ornaments,
by Jeff Paxton.
Patterns on pages 174–175

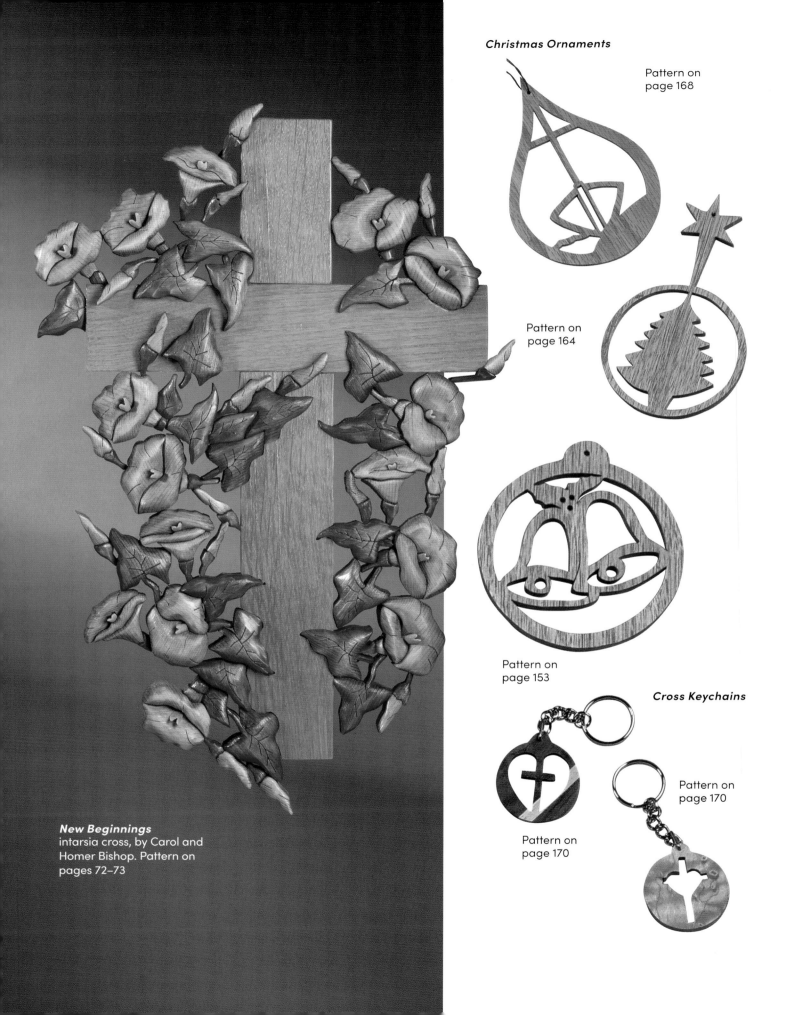

Christmas Ornaments

Pattern on page 168

Pattern on page 164

Pattern on page 153

Cross Keychains

Pattern on page 170

Pattern on page 170

New Beginnings
intarsia cross, by Carol and Homer Bishop. Pattern on pages 72–73

Nativity Display
3-D fretwork scene, by Carol and Homer Bishop. Try creating your smaller projects from CDs for a completely different look (right).

Communion Ornament,
Pattern on page 112

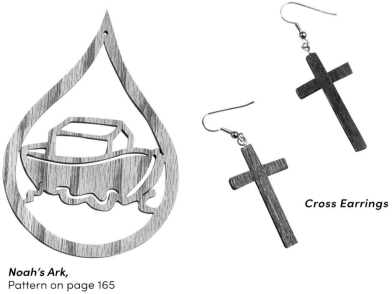

Noah's Ark,
Pattern on page 165

Cross Earrings

Getting Started

If you are new to scroll saw woodworking, it might seem daunting at the start. But it's actually one of the most beginner-friendly woodworking crafts out there and requires little in the way of startup costs. In this section, we'll cover the basic required tools, best practices, and key safety considerations.

Scroll Saw Basics

A scroll saw is an electrically powered saw with a reciprocating blade that moves up and down to cut through wood and other materials. One of the main advantages of a scroll saw is its removable blade, which you can easily insert into a predrilled hole and cut outward from the center of your project. Thanks to the scroll saw's versatility and ability to handle curves, tight corners, and tricky cuts, it is an excellent choice for creating beginner-friendly projects. Since the blade and saw are fixed, your job is to move the workpiece around, rather than moving the tool in relation to the workpiece. You're in control! Remember to go slow, have fun, and let the blade do the work.

Many scroll saws come with a light and a small air nozzle to help clear sawdust as you work. They also have mechanisms for controlling speed and cutting angle.

SELECTING A BLADE

Not only do blades come in different sizes, but the cutting teeth come in different configurations and different numbers of teeth per inch (TPI). As a general rule, the thickness of a blade increases as the numbers ascend; for instance, a #3 blade will have a smaller kerf than a #7 blade and be better suited for detail work, or thinner pieces of wood. You'll use two main blade types for your people and pet projects:

▶ Skip-Tooth

Skip-tooth blade.

Skip-tooth blades are the most common configuration. Instead of having one tooth right next to the last, they skip one tooth, leaving an open space between the teeth. The space helps clear sawdust and allows the blade to cut faster. Skip-tooth blades produce a slightly rougher cut surface, so you will likely need to sand after cutting.

▶ Reverse-Tooth

Reverse-tooth blade.

Reverse-tooth blades usually follow the skip-tooth or double-tooth configuration, but with the bottom couple of teeth pointed in the opposite direction from the rest. These teeth cut as the saw blade travels upward. Where skip-tooth and double-tooth blades splinter the bottom of the blank slightly, reverse-tooth blades remove these splinters. Reverse-tooth blades produce a cleaner bottom cut than other blades, but they don't clear as much sawdust. The sawdust can slow the cutting and possibly heat the blade, making it more likely to break or scorch the wood.

MATCHING WOOD TO BLADES

WOOD	THICKNESS	BLADE SIZE
Hardwood, softwood, plywood	¼" (6mm) or thinner	#2/0 to #1
Hardwood, softwood, plywood	¼" (6mm) to ½" (1.3cm)	#1 to #2
Hardwood, softwood, plywood	½" (1.3cm) to ¾" (1.9cm)	#3 to #4
Hardwood (less dense), softwood, plywood	¾" (1.9cm) to 1" (2.5cm)	#4 to #6
Hardwood (dense)	¾" (1.9cm) to 1" (2.5cm)	#5 to #7

Tools and Materials

Only a few tools are needed to complete the projects in this book—and they're probably already lying around your shop. You'll need a scroll saw and blades, your choice of wood, sanders for preparing and smoothing blanks, and a drill or drill press and bits.

- **Blue painter's tape, clear packaging tape, scroller's tape, shelf liner, temporary-bond spray adhesive, graphite or carbon transfer paper.** For attaching patterns to wood. Alternatively, use glue sticks instead of spray adhesive.
- **Finish of your choice.** Danish oil or mineral oil is common, but you can use a finish of your choice. Please note that some finishes are toxic, and follow all manufacturer's instructions.
- **Pencil or pen.** To mark measurements or trace patterns as needed.
- **Sandpaper.** For smoothing pieces of wood before and after scrolling.

Sanding Through the Grits

The grit number on a length of sandpaper refers to the average number of particles per square inch. The lower numbers, such as 60 and 80, are the coarser grits, which remove the most wood and are used for rough shaping. The higher numbers—220 and above—refer to finer grits that remove less wood and are used for smoothing. "Sanding through the grits" simply means using progressively finer sandpapers to smooth the scratches left by coarser grits. Rub sandpaper on a project until the wood is smooth and shaped the way you want. Then move on to a finer grit of paper and repeat, sanding with the grain when possible.

80 GRIT 120 GRIT 300 GRIT

CHOOSING WOOD

The following are some of the most common woods used in scroll saw woodworking.

 **Basswood:** This light, soft wood is consistent in grain and takes paint well, making it a great starter wood for beginners. Woodworkers based in Europe or the UK will find limewood to be a suitable substitute.

 **Cherry:** This hardwood has a rich, reddish hue and is similar to walnut in hardness. Cherry burns easily when cut with a power saw, so make sure to cover the wood with clear packaging tape before applying the pattern. In addition, you could use a large skip-tooth blade, as this can reduce the amount of dust that gets caught in the kerf (the cut path created by a blade).

 **Maple:** Dense and light in color with a distinctive grain, maple is highly prized by woodworkers. Just make sure to apply clear packaging tape to the surface of the wood before attaching a pattern, as maple can burn easily.

 **Pine:** Light-colored and beloved for its affordability and ubiquity, pine is a great starter wood for beginners to scrolling. However, it can be porous in places, increasing the chance of breakage on delicate projects.

 **Poplar:** Soft and easy to work with, poplar often takes on a slight greenish tinge once a finish is applied.

 **Walnut:** This durable wood is prized for its workability and deep, chocolatey color.

Safety

Take the time to properly prepare your workspace so your scrolling experience is safe and enjoyable. Work in a well-ventilated space and surround your setup with good, even lighting. Always wear a dust mask and safety goggles, tie up long hair, and secure loose clothing before beginning a project in your shop. When using power tools, such as drum sanders and band saws, employ a benchtop dust collector to help keep your work area clean and protect your lungs (see Sidebar below) to ensure that you can scroll without difficulty for years to come.

Why is Wood Dust a Health Concern?

Wood dust is considered carcinogenic to humans. Exposure to certain kinds of wood dust has been associated with health issues due to the natural chemicals in the wood, or substances in the wood, such as bacteria, mold, and fungi. Wood dust is also associated with irritation of the eyes, nose, and throat; dermatitis; and respiratory system effects, including decreased lung capacity and allergic reactions. It is imperative to wear personal protective equipment while working with wood. Always research a wood's toxicity before beginning any project.

Special Considerations

CUTTING PUZZLES AND PUZZLE ORNAMENTS

Puzzles should be made from good-quality hardwood plywood that is ¼" (6.4mm) thick. Use two layers of wood—the top layer being of birch or maple plywood and the bottom layer of a less expensive material. Making these puzzles is an easy process. Cut the puzzle pieces out of the top layer. Glue the remaining border to the bottom layer to form a frame with backing for the puzzle pieces. You can finish the puzzles with whatever you'd like!

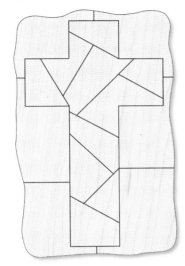

Pattern on page 209.

The **puzzle ornaments** in this book will require a ³⁄₃₂" (2.4mm) drill bit. Because of the thin parts on some of the ornaments, I recommend using a plywood that is ³⁄₈" (9.5mm) thick. Additionally, you will need a drill with a ³⁄₃₂" (2.4mm) bit to drill hanging holes.

To cut the ornaments out, a skip-tooth blade will work well. Select a blade with 11.5 to 12.5 teeth per inch and a size of #3 to #7. Small blades are better suited for thinner, lighter workpieces; large blades are better suited to thicker, denser ones. Each ornament requires a ³⁄₃₂" (2.4mm) hole drilled down through the center. The centerline is indicated by a dashed line on each pattern. Although some ornaments can be drilled prior to cutting, many will require cutting the ornament first. Then, drill as far as the bit will allow, remove the drilled pieces, and then drill some more. A standard-length bit will work fine, but an extended length bit will allow for the maximum spindle travel of the drill press.

When making these ornaments or designing your own, remember the centerline must penetrate each individual piece of the ornament. All the ornament pieces are held together by the string used for hanging the ornament.

Some of the ornaments require cutting sharp inside corners. Spin the workpiece around the blade to make these cuts. The best way to cut sharp corners is to stand directly in front of the saw and feed the material steadily into the blade. When a sharp turn is required, reduce the feeding pressure while spinning the workpiece sharply around the blade. Do not put pressure sideways on the blade. When the pattern lines up with the front of the blade, begin feeding the material again.

After cutting the ornaments out, sand the edges smooth with 100-grit sandpaper. Then sand the entire ornament with 220-grit sandpaper prior to painting. You may paint and decorate ornaments with acrylic colors. A suitable string or cord loop (knotted at the bottom) has to be inserted through the hole to hang the ornament. An easy way to string the ornament is to first assemble all of the pieces. Then, insert a fine piece of piano wire or similar with a small hook on the end through the hole from the top and all the way through to the bottom. Hook the top of the string loop and pull it up through the hole. A small amount of glue at the top of the hole will keep the string in place and prevent the ornament from falling apart.

Pattern on page 187.

Message Through Design

Symbolism

The use of symbols to convey abstract ideas is as old as the world. With no printed word, cultures relied upon symbols to communicate. A variety of languages and dialects within a language also dictated the need for universal symbols.

Many of the Christian symbols that were developed hundreds of years ago to tell the story of Christ still have meaning today. They are found in traditions and teachings, on church windows and furnishings.

This book describes some of the more common symbols. Others exist.

Symbolism is a universal language that expresses abstract ideas through suggestion. The word symbol is derived from the two Greek words, *syn*, meaning "together," and *ballein*, meaning "to throw." The symbolon, or symbol, becomes a mark that joins together an abstract idea and a likeness to an object or experience. Through association, the mark, no matter how trivial, becomes a story much deeper than meets the eye.

The language of symbols served a real need in the early Christian church. There was no printed word. Also, there was a variety of languages and dialects. Christians depended on symbolic language to recapture the story of Christ and his promises. They also used symbols to provide a secret language during periods of persecution.

Today, symbolism is still an important part of the elements of Christian faith, tradition, and teachings. The use of symbols on church windows and furnishings present an interesting and valuable pictorial supplement to preaching and religious education.

Christians have utilized many different symbols to proclaim their faith. To give a complete description of those symbols would require more pages than is the intent of this book. Included here are only those symbols which are used in the design of the patterns in this book.

Although many symbols are religious symbols, it is important to remember that a "religious" symbol is not necessarily a "Christian" symbol. Symbolism is as old as the world and many symbols belong to pagan religions. Before the development of any "Christian" design, verification should be made of the symbols used and their association with the Christian faith. In using Christian forms and symbols, three worthy virtues of their use should be noted: reverence, simplicity, and sincerity.

This book may be used as a reference for some of the more common symbols. Other symbols may be discovered by reading the writings of the prophets.

NUMBERS

Numbers have significance in most cultures. The Bible also contains many examples of symbolic numbers. The following are the most common numbers and some of their symbolisms.

ONE: Unity; oneness; God.

TWO: Refers to the dual nature of Christ (human and divine). It is also the division of unity; duality; and opposites.

THREE: The Holy Trinity; body, mind, and spirit; beginning, middle, and end; the threefold of nature (lower or animal, human, and spiritual or higher).

FOUR: Representative of the material things, such as the four elements (earth, air, fire, and water).

FIVE: The five senses of man; the five wounds of Christ.

SIX: The six days of Creation.

SEVEN: The seven days of the week; the seven heavens; the seven gifts of the Holy Spirit (traditionally wisdom, understanding, counsel, might, knowledge, piety, and fear of the Lord).

EIGHT: The number of the octave—rebirth; regeneration at Baptism; the Resurrection; the eight Beatitudes (Christ's promises of coming blessings).

NINE: The number nine hardly appears. There are nine orders of angels. Nine is a completion (nine months from conception to birth). The gates of Hell are thrice threefold: three of brass, three of iron, and three of adamantine rock. When the fallen angels were expelled from Heaven, they fell in nine days.

TEN: The perfect number; the number of commandments. Also the ten petals of the passion flower; a mystical meaning of the Apostles, because of the twelve, one denied the Lord and one betrayed him.

TWELVE: The twelve prophets and the twelve disciples; the number of months in a year.

THIRTEEN: Considered unlucky because it was the number of people at the Last Supper, where one betrayed Jesus.

FIFTEEN: Progress; the number of steps the Virgin Mary ascended when she entered the Temple on leaving her parents.

FORTY: A period of trial; as used in the Bible, it refers to a "long time" or a "great many," not necessarily an exact number.

CROSSES

The simplest cross is an upright stake having one or more cross pieces. Used in the time of Abraham as a method of capital punishment, it became an image of pain, guilt, and disgrace.

After Christ was crucified on the cross, Christians adopted it to signify a servant and follower of Christ. That meaning continues today. The cross also signifies redemption through the death and resurrection of Jesus.

In wider terms, the cross represents the union of the opposites because of the horizontal cross pieces joined to vertical ones.

The cross belongs to no one religious denomination. More than 400 various shapes of the cross exist today. This book includes only a small portion of that number.

OTHER SYMBOLS

Anchor: A secret sign of the early church, with the cross as part of the anchor. If the church is a ship, it must have an anchor.

Angel: The most misunderstood and abused subject in Christian art. Messengers of God, angels should be properly represented as beardless, sexless winged beings in human form with bare feet. Angels are spirits created by God before the world to serve him. Although they exist in a different dimension from the physical, visible world we know, they may assume bodies. Angels are often shown with hands folded in prayer or with a right hand extended to indicate guardianship of humans or God's protective love. The Christmas (herald) angels symbolize God's redeeming love; angels shown with trumpets suggest praise of God or proclamation of his name. They are used as symbols of the Last Day.

Apple: Represents the fall of man. It also symbolizes man's temptation or attraction to the material world.

Ark: An ark floating upon the stormy waters symbolizes the church riding in safety amidst the world's struggles and tribulations. It shelters the faithful from the flood.

Bell: Represents a call to worship. It also signifies the preacher who, like a bell, encourages the faithful.

Book: The Bible, symbolic of authoritative wisdom or learning. An open book represents a relevant prophecy or saying.

Bread & Symbols of Holy Communion: As a symbol of the body of Christ, bread is the source of man's redemption. In sharing the bread, the communicants become one in and with the body of Christ. The chalice or cup holds the wine, or the blood of Christ.

Butterfly: A symbol of the resurrection and eternal life. The three stages of the butterfly—caterpillar, larva, and butterfly—parallel terrestrial life, death, and final celestial destination.

Candle: Symbolizes Christ as the "Light of the World" and humans' aspiration for the source of all light and life. The number of candles also has significance:

> **One:** Unity
> **Two:** The dual natures of Christ—human and divine
> **Three:** Holy Trinity
> **Four:** Advent
> **Five:** Five wounds of Christ
> **Seven:** The seven gifts of the Spirit, the Seven Sacraments

Christmas Tree: Because the tree remains green throughout the winter when most plants die, evergreens remain a symbol of life. The tree symbolizes the Garden of Eden's "Tree of Life." Also, the star on the Christmas tree reminds us of the star of Bethlehem, "the Light of the World."

Church: Because Christians found refuge in the church, the ship became an early symbol for the church. The steeple or spire points heavenward. The steps or stairs at the entrance symbolize the pathway to God's ways. The large open doors of the church invite all people inside.

Crown: The crown reminds us of Christ's victory over sin and death. It is a symbol of the divine nature of Jesus Christ.

Crucifix: Not a symbol, but a representative of Christ suspended on the cross.

Dove: A descending dove is probably the most universal symbol of the Holy Spirit. A dove with an olive branch symbolizes peace from the reconciliation between God and man. The dove with a drop of water symbolizes God using earthly water and divine spirit to create life out of chaos. A dove with flames is symbolic of the fire of the Holy Spirit at Pentecost. Seven flames represent the seven gifts of the Spirit.

Emmanuel: This word is a combination of three Hebrew words which mean "God with us."

Fire/Flame: Next to the dove, this is the most common symbol of the Holy Spirit. It represents destruction and regeneration, such as the "flames of Hell" or the "tongues of fire" associated with the Holy Spirit. It also represents Jesus as the "Light of the World." Seven flames refer to the seven gifts of the Spirit.

Fish: Also called the ichthys symbol. Used in times of persecution as a secret sign by which Christians identified themselves to other Christians. The Greek word for fish formed an acrostic of the Greek phrase "Jesus Christ, God's Son, Savior." The symbol provided protection from non-Christians, and when drawn on the walls of underground passageways directed worshippers to meeting places. A single fish represents the Savior while several fish represent faithful Christians.

Folded Hands: Symbolic of prayer.

Greenery: Used as a symbol of eternal life.

Hand of God: When the hand of God proceeds from the clouds, a triradiate nimbus usually surrounds it. It is suggestive of the presence and sympathy of the Holy Trinity.

Heart: Reminds us of God's love for his people and the love of Christians for one another. The "Sacred Heart of Jesus" is symbolized by a heart pierced with three nails and encircled by the crown of thorns. A heart pierced by a sword symbolizes the Virgin Mary.

Holly: The thorns of the holly leaves symbolize the suffering of Jesus on the cross.

Hosanna: The Greek form of the Hebrew petition "Save, we beseech Thee."

Key: The key symbolizes the keys to the kingdom of heaven.

Lamb of God: Or *Agnus Dei*, one of the oldest symbols known to the church. The banner shows us Jesus victorious over death. Sometimes the symbol is pictured on a book with seven seals. Other times there are four rivers for the Gospel flowing from four books.

Lamp/Lantern: Symbolizes wisdom or knowledge. It is also a symbol of Christ. As stated in Psalms 119:105, "Thy word is a lamp unto my feet, and a light unto my path."

Lily: A symbol of the Virgin Mary and the state of purity and chastity attributed to her. It reminds us that Jesus was born of a virgin mother.

Manger: The manger, which is a feeding trough, has become a symbol of our Lord's nativity. The manger is sometimes depicted empty and sometimes with the Holy Child in it. A nimbus surrounds his head.

Nimbus: From the Latin word for "cloud"; it is a circle of light surrounding the head of a saint. It is not a halo. It is sometimes shown with three rays from the center (triradiate). A symbol of serenity or great distinction in the church, the rayed nimbus should be used only to symbolize God or a person of the Holy Trinity.

Noel: From the Latin word natalis, which means "relating to birth." It now refers to the birth of Christ, or the Christmas season.

Palm Branch: Symbolizes triumph and victory over death and Christ's entry into Jerusalem. It is also a symbol of martyrdom.

Rainbow: Symbolizes a reconciliation between God and man. God set it in the heavens as a promise that floods will never come again.

Rose: A symbol of the Messiah; Jesus' mother, Mary; and Christ's human birth and humility. The red rose that sprang from Christ's blood shed on Calvary represents love and martyrdom.

Shell: The scallop shell has become the symbol of baptism and pilgrimage. The shell and water united remind us of our birth as God's children through baptism.

Ship: Symbolic of the church under the leadership of Christ. The church is the vessel of spiritual guidance for sailing over the sea or waters of life.

Star: Symbol of the divine light. The star shining in the night represents the Holy Spirit penetrating the darkness. The nativity star heralds the birth of Christ.

 Cross Star: A four-point star.

 Bethlehem Star: A five-point star (Epiphany Star, Star of Jessie).

Creator's Star: A six-point star, symbolic of the six days of creation (Star of David).

Mystic Star: A seven-point star. Represents the seven gifts of the Holy Spirit.

Star of Regeneration: An eight-point star (star of baptism).

Fruits of the Spirit Star: A nine-point star.

Star of the Apostles: A twelve-point star (star for the twelve tribes).

Steeple: Pointing upward, where Christ sits at the right hand of God the Father.

Sun: It is masculine, as opposed to the moon, which is feminine. A sign of the joy and hope that dispels the darkness and despair of sin, the sun symbolizes Christ's resurrection.

Sword: The symbol of power and authority, it is linked to the cross by its shape.

Torch: The torch signifies Christian witnessing: "Let your light so shine before men, that they may see your good works, and glorify your Father which is in heaven" (Matthew 5:16).

Tree: As a counterpart to the ladder and the pillar, the tree is symbolic of the link between heaven and earth. The tree's three main divisions (roots, trunk, and branches) also correspond to the three divisions of man (body, mind, and spirit).

Water: A symbol of holy baptism, water is a source of life. It is also symbolic of an inner or higher truth, rather than the outer literal significance of the rock.

Whale: Symbolic of the tomb from which men will emerge, overcoming death to have eternal life.

Window: The window is inseparable from the symbolism of light.

SYMBOLISM OF COLOR

Colors also speak symbolically of the Christian faith. For those interested in painting any portion of their design, the following provides information on color variation and its meaning.

( ) - Denotes traditional association with the Western world.

Black: Denotes mourning, grief, sorrow, death, and

remembrance. (Sin, death, evil)

Blue: Suggests good health, eternity, and heaven. (Hope, love, truth, faithfulness, heaven)

Brown: The color of the earth, happiness.

Green: Green is the universal color of nature. It is also the color of life, growth innocence, freshness, and a symbol for the Holy Trinity. (Growth, victory, hope)

Orange: Ambition, endurance.

Purple: Ancient color of royalty. Faith, trust, penitence. It is equally appropriate to be used in lieu of violet.

Red: A color for the Holy Spirit. It represents humanity, love, bravery, and trust. It also refers to the blood of the martyrs of the church. (Fire, love)

Royal Blue: Trust.

Scarlet: (Royalty, loyalty)

Violet: Suggests penitence, sorrow, humility, suffering, sympathy, and fasting. (Royalty, repentance, remorse)

White: Symbolic of gladness, glory, light, joy, and purity. White is the color of the Creator. (Purity, holiness, innocence, faith, light)

Yellow/Gold: Represents the glory of God, the might of his people, and wisdom. Gold:(God's abundance, marriage)

Church Calendar Colors: Certain colors have become associated with the church year. Listed below are the major and minor church festivals and special occasions along with their symbolic color.

  Advent: Violet or blue.

  New Year's Eve/Day: White.

  Epiphany: White
  (Second through Eighth Sundays—green).

  Transfiguration of our Lord: White.

  Ash Wednesday: Violet or black.

  Lent: Violet.

  Palm Sunday: Scarlet or violet.

Maundy Thursday: Scarlet or white.

Good Friday: Black.

Easter: White (Easter Day—white or gold).

Pentecost: Red.

Trinity Sunday: White.

Season after Pentecost: Green.

Reformation days: Red.

All Saints' Day: White.

Thanksgiving Day: White.

Although many of the designs in this book are self-explanatory, some designs incorporate several symbols to convey a special meaning. Some of the designs included in this book are listed below along with the intended messages.

Weddings and Anniversaries: The two banded rings in these designs symbolize the couple being united into one flesh. The linked rings show that Christ binds the couple together in love. When these banded rings are intertwined in a symbol for Christ, such as a cross, Chi Rho, dove, circle, or Cross of Constantine, the rings become symbolic of a desire to have Christ as the center of the couple's life together.

The cross represents the union of opposites and reminds us of the ultimate sacrificial love. The dove represents the presence of God through the Holy Spirit. The heart symbolizes the promise a couple makes before God. The butterfly is symbolic of the couple's beginning a new life together through Christian marriage, while the plant represents the believers who know that new life begins in Christ. The circle is used in these designs to suggest unity and eternity.

Baptism in Christ: The shell and water united together symbolize the sacrament of baptism. The dove represents meekness, purity, and the splendor of righteousness and is symbolic of the Holy Spirit. Three drops of water are used to remind us that the ceremony is done in the name of the Father, the Son, and the Holy Spirit.

Lamb of God: The halo around the lamb distinguishes it as the "Lamb of God," who was sacrificed on the cross for the forgiveness of sins.

Church on a Rock: According to Matthew 16:18, "Upon this rock I will build my church; and the gates of Hell shall not prevail against it." Those who hear the words of God and follow them will be like the wise man who built his house upon a rock, a secure foundation.

Christ with Open Arms: All people are welcomed to accept salvation through faith in Christ.

Cross/Chalice/Bread: The bread (host) and wine (chalice) symbolize the body and blood of Christ, shed on the cross for the forgiveness of sins.

Chalice/Bread/Candle: The bread and wine (the body and blood of Christ) are united together in communion for the forgiveness of sins and renewed strength in faith.

Star/Cross/Crown/Manger: The star's rays descend to form the manger. The newborn king and those who came to worship him are represented by the crown which is above the manger.

Epiphany Chi Rho: The first two letters of Christ, in Greek, combined to form a symbol representing Christ's birth. A manger is formed with a nimbus above it.

Advent Candles: Symbolizes the four Sundays of Advent. The cross, berries, and the thorns of the holly leaves remind us of Christ's suffering on the cross, where he shed his blood for the forgiveness of sins.

Crosses

Patterns throughout this book are 100% of size unless otherwise indicated.

Calvary Trio Cross
This pattern captures the solemn narrative of Golgotha, where three crosses stood for Christ and the two thieves. Its design is a stark reminder of the sacrifice and redemption offered on that fateful day, encapsulating a pivotal moment in Christian faith.

Cross in Eternity
This design symbolizes the eternal and unending nature of Christ's love.

Dove Cross
This design symbolizes peace, purity, and the descent of the Holy Spirit into the realm of man, as recounted in the scriptures.

Floral Fretwork Cross, by Tim Andrews.

Cross of Constantine
Christ the Conquering King. This cross is the Chi Rho except with the "X" turned to form the cross.

Budded Cross
Also called the Cross Treflée or
Cross Bontonée. The three circles
(trefoil) at the end of each arm
symbolize the Holy Trinity.

Cross in Glory #1
Also called the Easter Cross or
Rayed Cross. The Latin-type cross
has Easter lilies surrounding it
or rays of light from a rising sun.
The rising sun symbolizes the
conquering of death by Jesus'
resurrection.

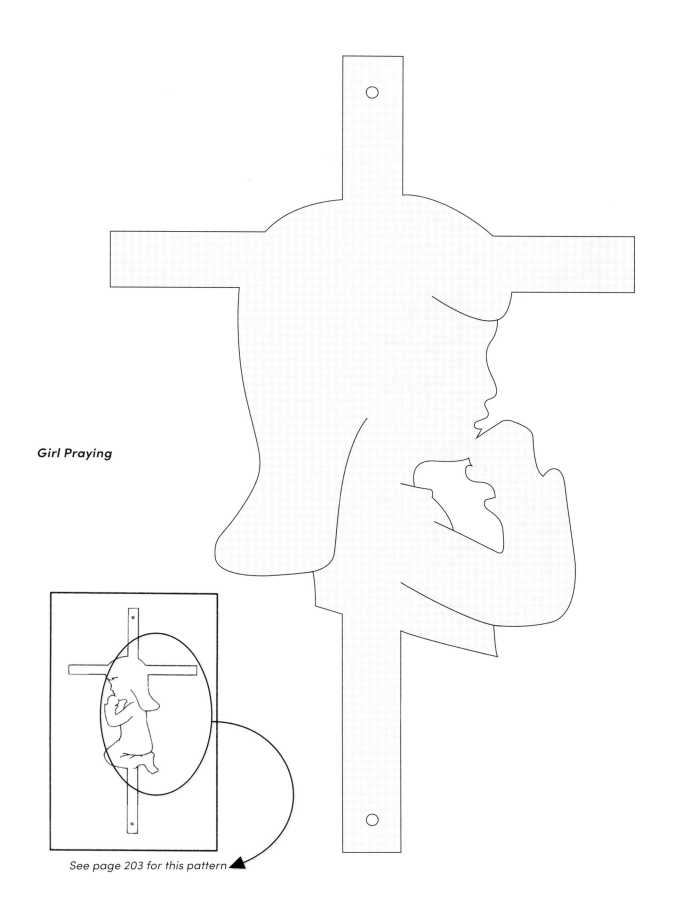

Girl Praying

See page 203 for this pattern

Boy Praying

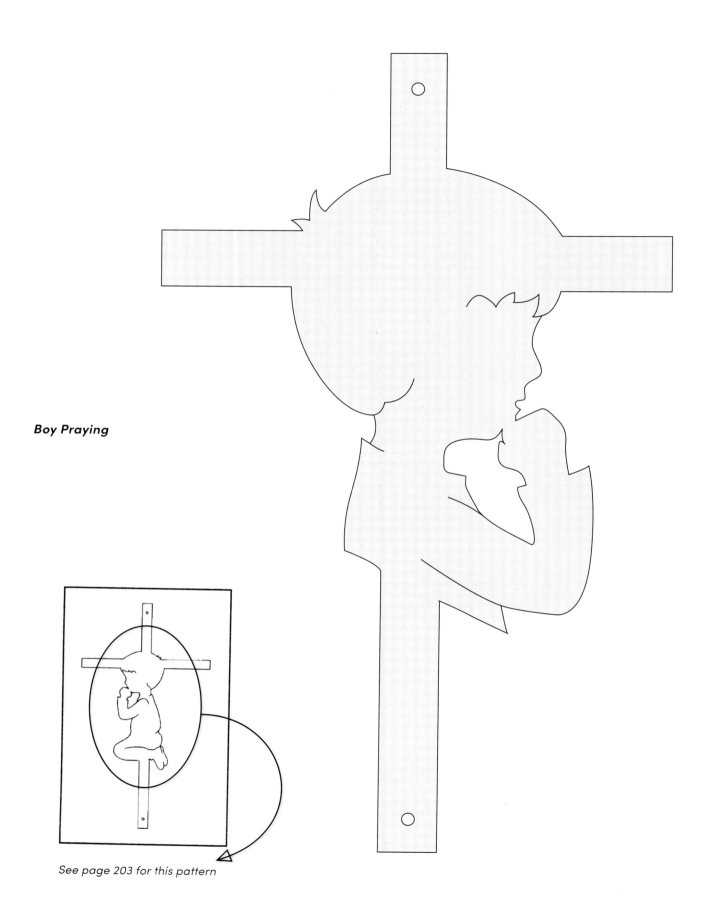

See page 203 for this pattern

Cross in Glory #2

Cross in Glory #3

Cross in Glory: Lily

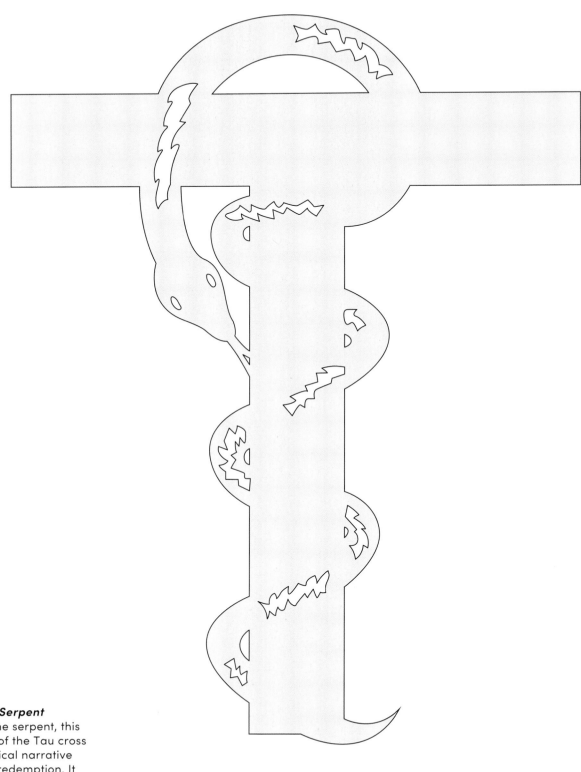

Tau Cross with Serpent
Enveloped by the serpent, this
representation of the Tau cross
reflects the biblical narrative
of healing and redemption. It
signifies the transformative power
of faith and divine deliverance
from sin.

The Cross and Thorny Crown
This cross is a slender Latin-type cross with an interlaced crown of thorns. It is symbolic of passion.

Mission Cross
A cross in the shape
of a fishhook for Jesus'
commandment to his
followers that they become
"fishers of men."

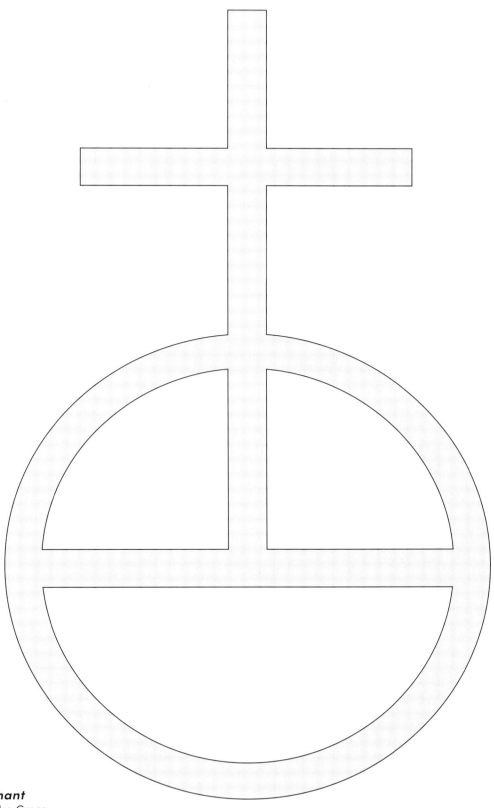

Cross Triumphant
Also known as the Cross of Victory or the Cross of Conquest. This cross represents a world united in Christ.

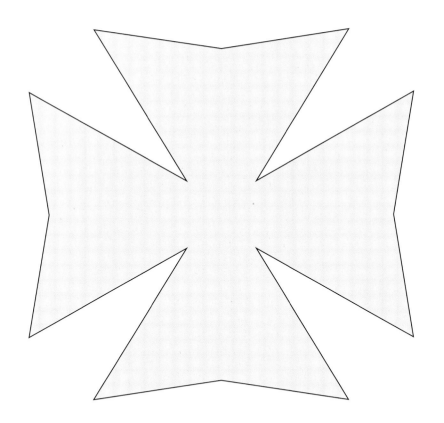

Maltese Cross
An emblem of John the Baptist and the Knights of St. John. The cross has four arms of equal length. The arms are slanted lines rather than curved. With two points on each arm, it represents the eight Beatitudes.

Cross Fleurie
A cross of the Latin or Greek type. At the end of each arm is a petal-like point.

Cross Fleur-de-Lis
At the end of each large arm is a fleur-de-lis.

Trinity Cross
Similar to the Cross Fleur-de-Lis, but much more intricate and beautiful. At the end of each arm are three fleur-de-lis.

Cross and Crown
Symbolizes a reward to those who are faithful unto death. Palm branches surround the cross and crown, alluding to Jesus' triumphant entry into Jerusalem.

Shepherd's Crook Cross
The shepherd's crook symbolizes Jesus as the Good Shepherd. This cross reminds us who laid down his life for the sheep.

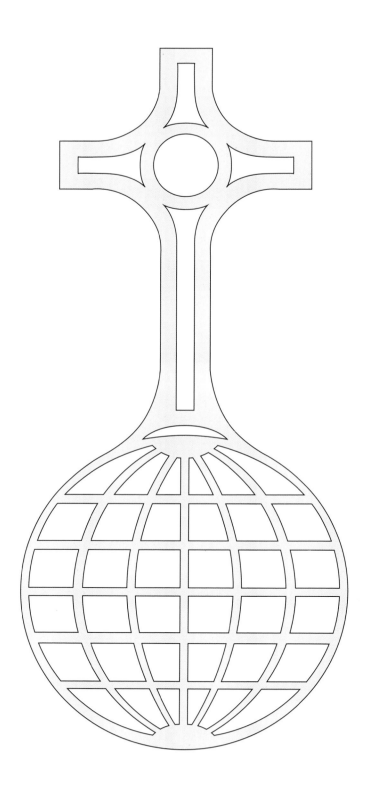

Cross Over the World
A cross reigns over the world, represented by the ball. This cross symbolizes the triumph of Jesus over the sins of the world.

Cross Crosslet

This cross consists of four Latin crosses with their lower arms joined at the center. It is symbolic of the spread of Christianity to the four corners of the earth.

Jerusalem Cross

Four Tau crosses meet to form a large cross (it symbolizes the five wounds of the Lord). The four small crosses symbolize the four corners of the earth to which missionaries have carried the gospel.

Love-Engrained Cross
This cross, adorned with hearts from base to tip, symbolizes the permeating love that forms the core of Christian teaching. Each heart is a reminder of love's guiding principle in faith and life.

Unity Cross
With interlocking rings and a central orb, this cross represents the bond of fellowship among believers and the eternal nature of divine promises, encapsulating the unity and continuity of Christian community through time.

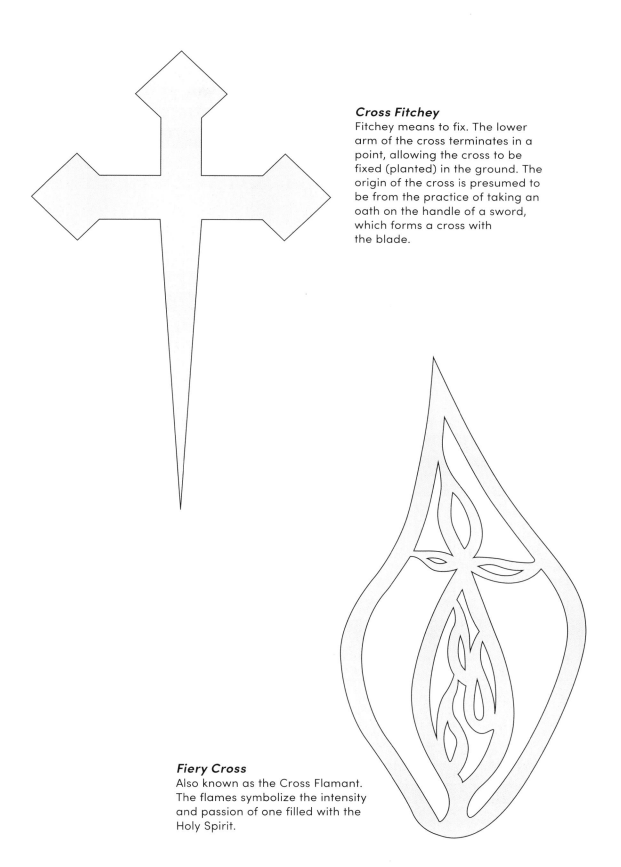

Cross Fitchey

Fitchey means to fix. The lower arm of the cross terminates in a point, allowing the cross to be fixed (planted) in the ground. The origin of the cross is presumed to be from the practice of taking an oath on the handle of a sword, which forms a cross with the blade.

Fiery Cross

Also known as the Cross Flamant. The flames symbolize the intensity and passion of one filled with the Holy Spirit.

Greek Cross and Chi
It symbolizes the inseparability of Christ and the cross. The Greek letter "X" (Chi) represents the first letter of Christ and is combined with the cross.

Cross Patonce
Similar to the Cross Fleurie. The arms on this cross gradually and gracefully curve out toward the three petals.

Crucifix

Figure to be glued to the cross

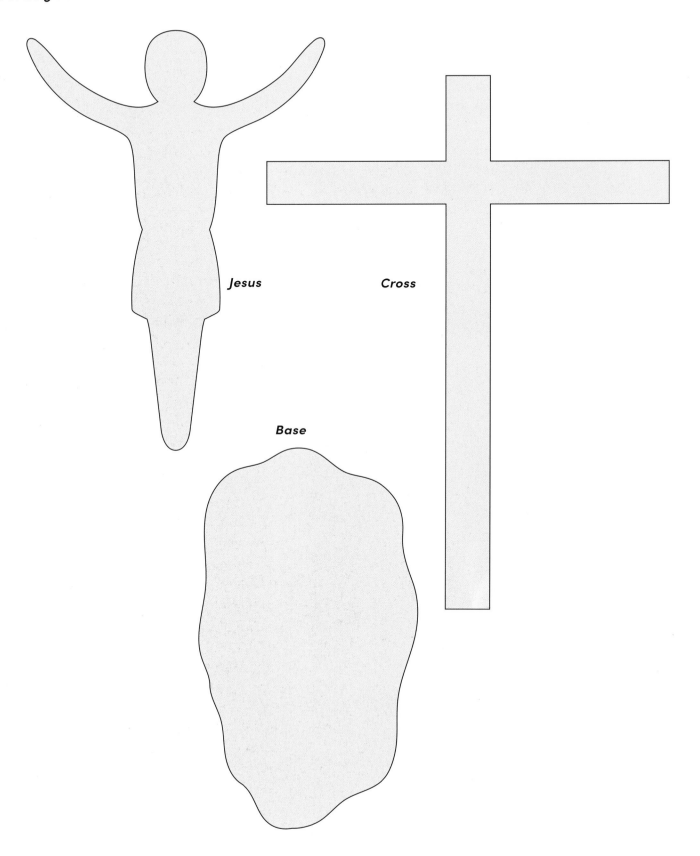

Jesus

Cross

Base

Butterfly Cross
Butterflies are widely regarded as symbols of resurrection, transformation, and the soul.

Praying Hands

Triune Cross
The dots on each arm here represent the Triune God.

Saltire Cross
The repeated Xs within the larger shape represent Saint Andrew's request to be crucified on a diagonal cross as a sign of respect for Christ.

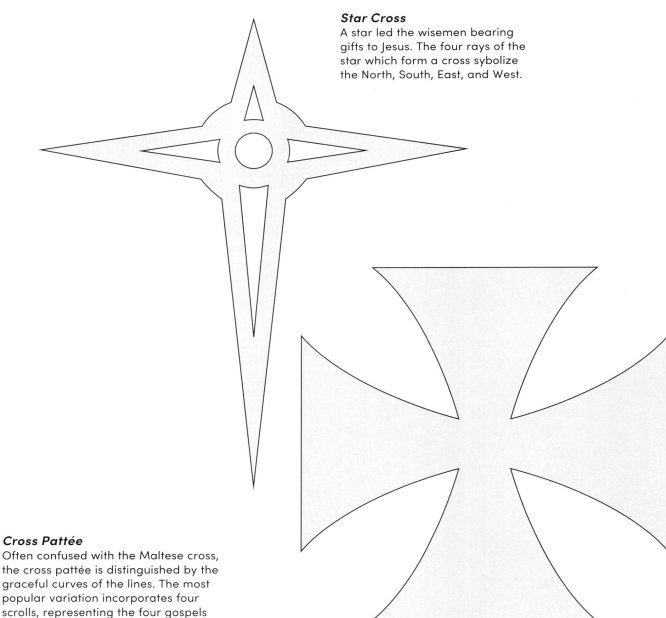

Star Cross

A star led the wisemen bearing gifts to Jesus. The four rays of the star which form a cross sybolize the North, South, East, and West.

Cross Pattée

Often confused with the Maltese cross, the cross pattée is distinguished by the graceful curves of the lines. The most popular variation incorporates four scrolls, representing the four gospels (one in each corner). The Gospel Mathew is represented by a winged man (stressing the Lord's human nature), Mark by a winged lion, Luke by a winged ox, and John by a winged eagle. The wings represent the divine inspiration of the four accounts of Jesus' time on earth. The scrolls should be positioned as follows:

Mathew–upper left
Mark–lower left
Luke–lower right
John–upper right

Crosses

Part 4
Cut4

Part 1

Star of Bethlehem,
3-D Victorian fretwork ornament.

Part 3

Part 2

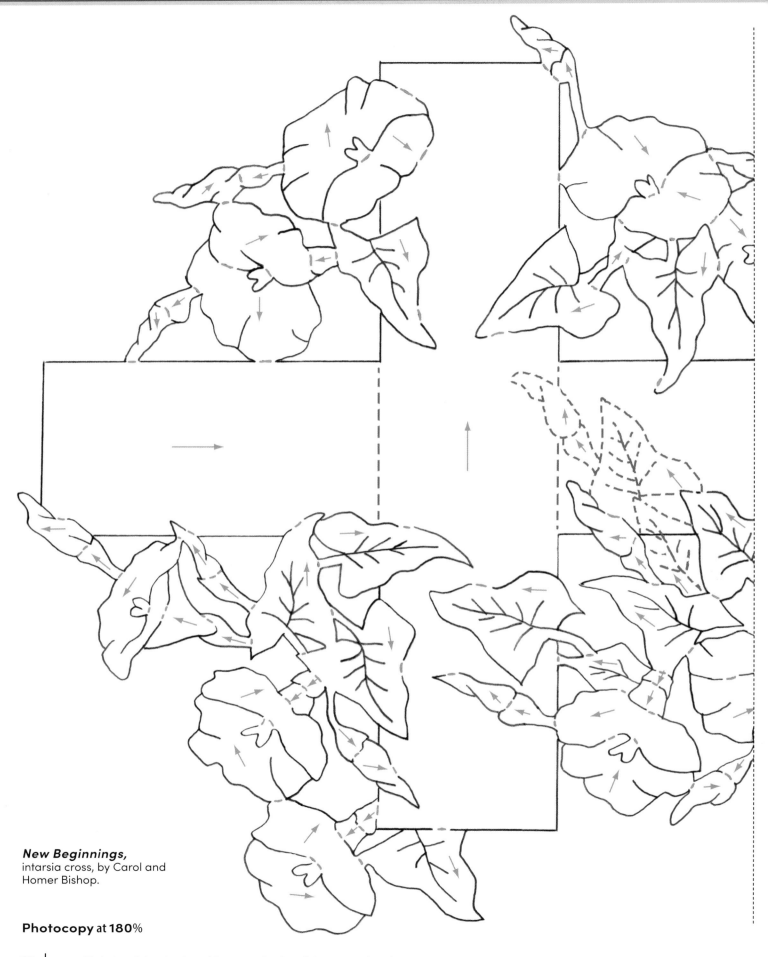

New Beginnings,
intarsia cross, by Carol and
Homer Bishop.

Photocopy at **180**%

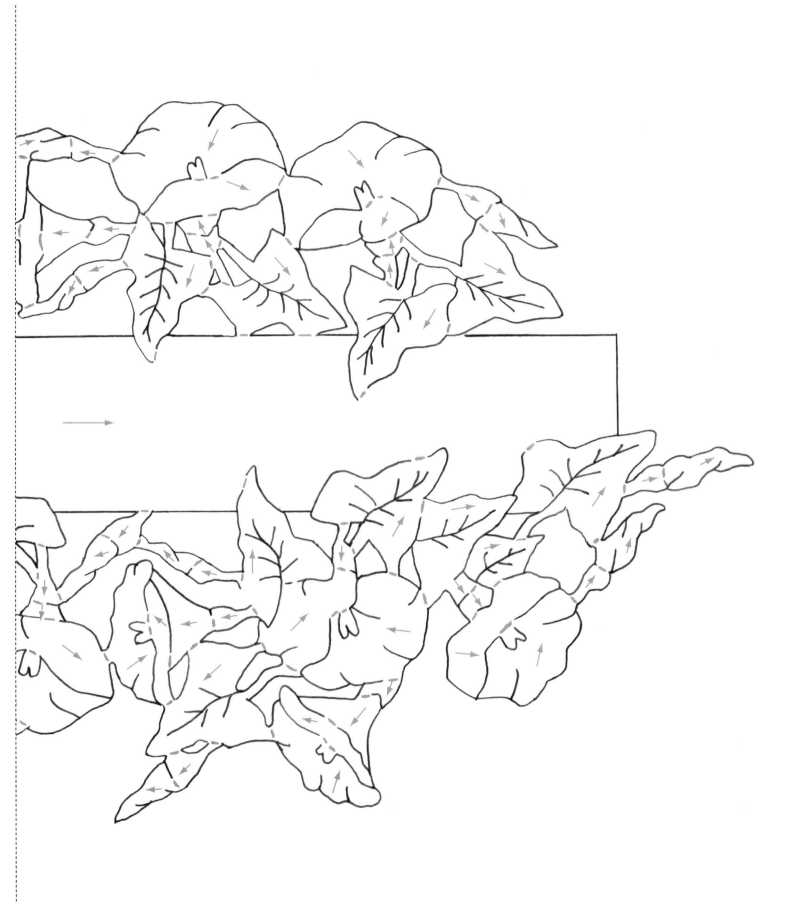

Symbol of Faith,
Victorian cross, by John A. Nelson and
Ben Fink.

Photocopy at 165%

Plaques, Signs, and Lettering

Pilot Me Plaque

Matthew 28:20

I am the Light of the World

John 8:12

I am the Resurrection and the Life

John 11:25

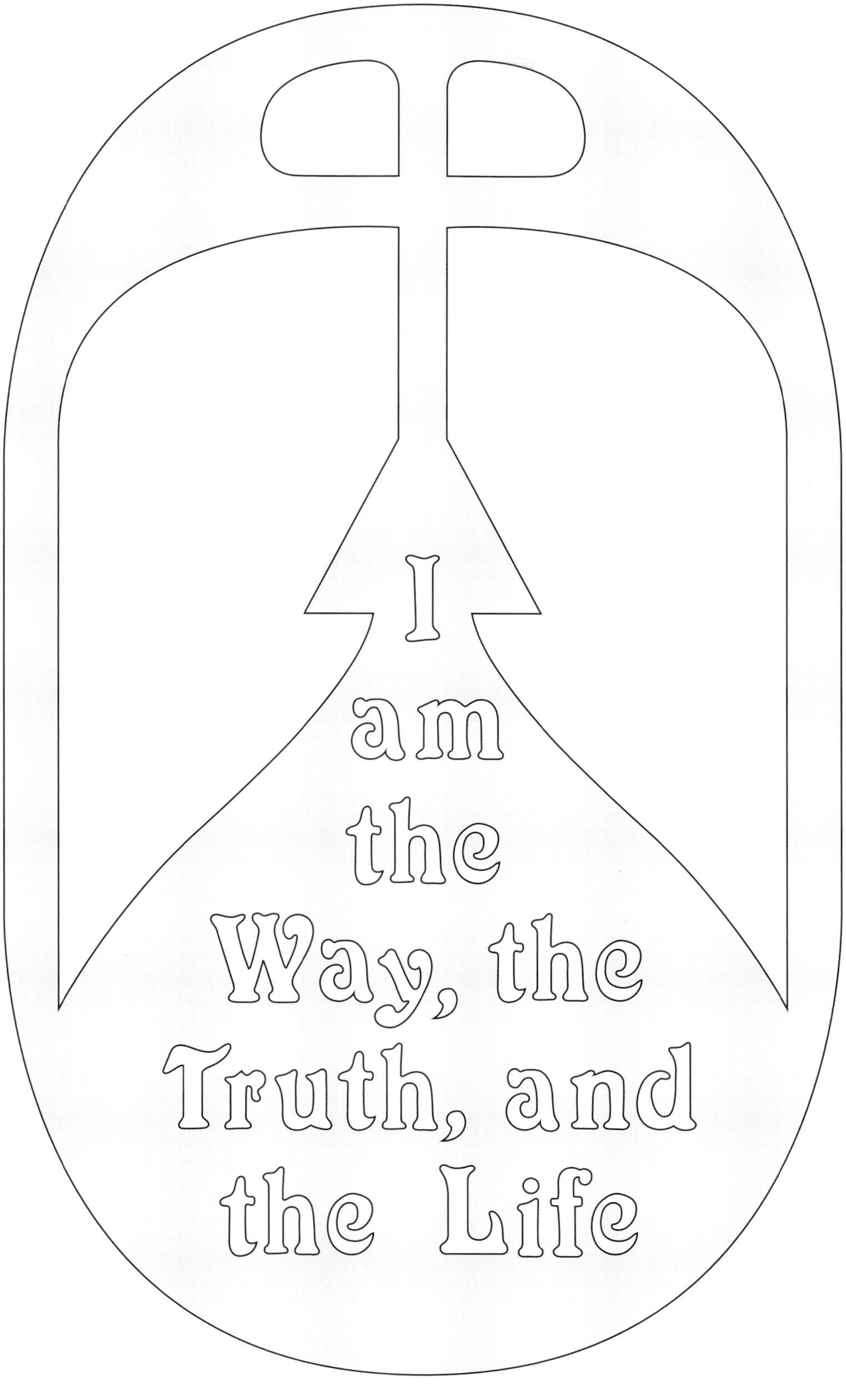
I
am
the
Way, the
Truth, and
the Life

John 14:6

John 15:5

Love, Peace, Joy Sign

Matthew 28:6

**Bless Our
Home Sign**

God Bless You Sign

**Bless This
House Sign**

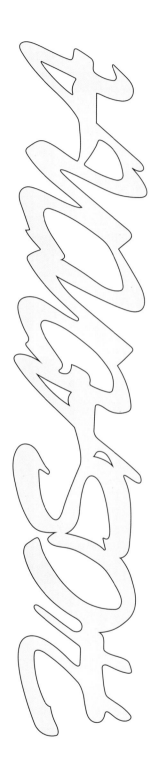

Hosanna Sign/
Appliqué

We Will Serve Sign

Dove Peace Appliqué

**Joy, Crosses,
Love Appliqués**

Note: Customize the pattern at the left by substituting the patterns above

Bless This House Lettering

Praise the Lord Lettering

Love Appliqué

Bless Our Home Lettering

Ecclesiastes 3:1

Jesus Is #1 Sign

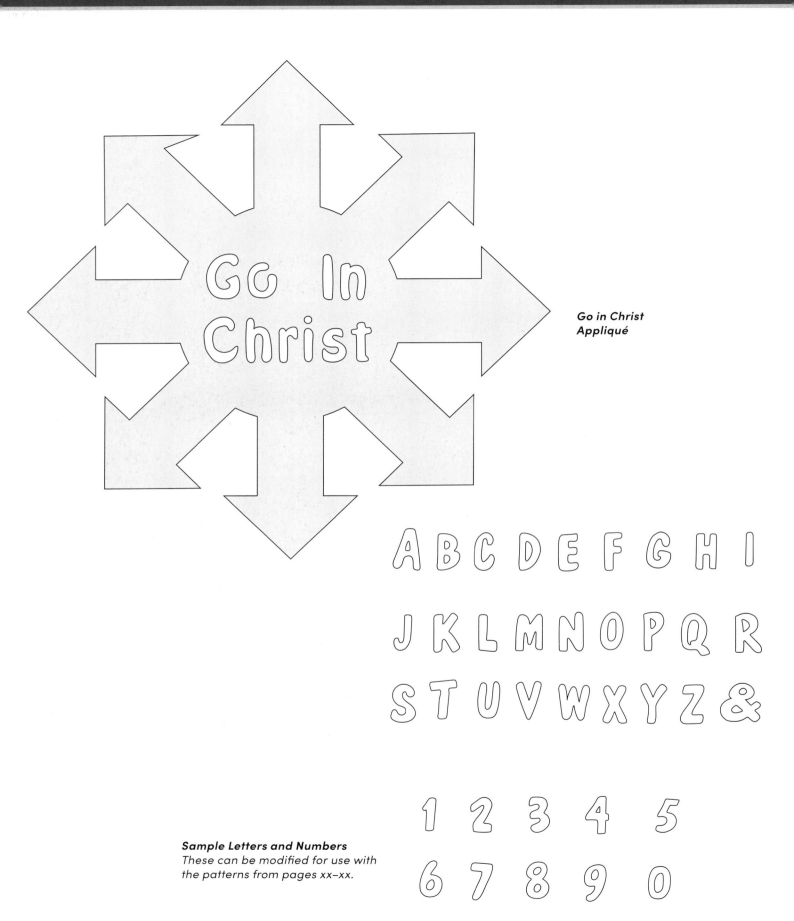

**Go in Christ
Appliqué**

A B C D E F G H I

J K L M N O P Q R

S T U V W X Y Z &

1 2 3 4 5

6 7 8 9 0

Sample Letters and Numbers
These can be modified for use with the patterns from pages xx–xx.

ANDREA MARGARET

OCT 8 1978

BAPTIZED IN CHRIST

REBECCA LYNN

MAY 10 1981

BAPTIZED IN CHRIST

Personalized Ornaments

Personalized Marriage Sign

*Thanks be to
God Sign*

Boy Praying Sign

Girl Praying Sign

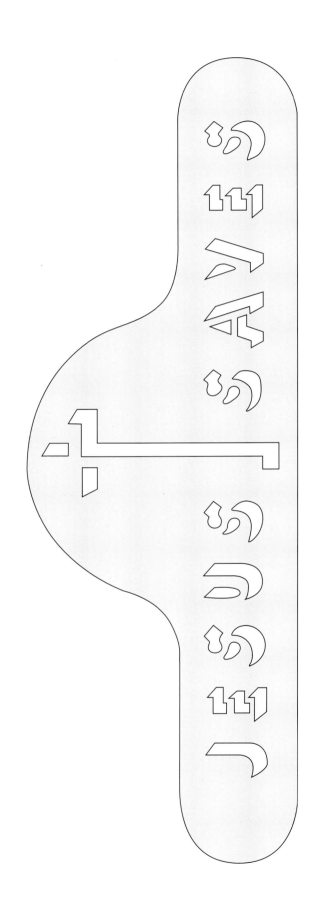

Jesus Saves Plaque

Daily Bread Sign

Give Thanks Sign

Peace Appliqué & Ornament

Welcome Sign

Torch

The Lamb of God

Church on Rock

Jesus and Children

*Communion
with Cross*

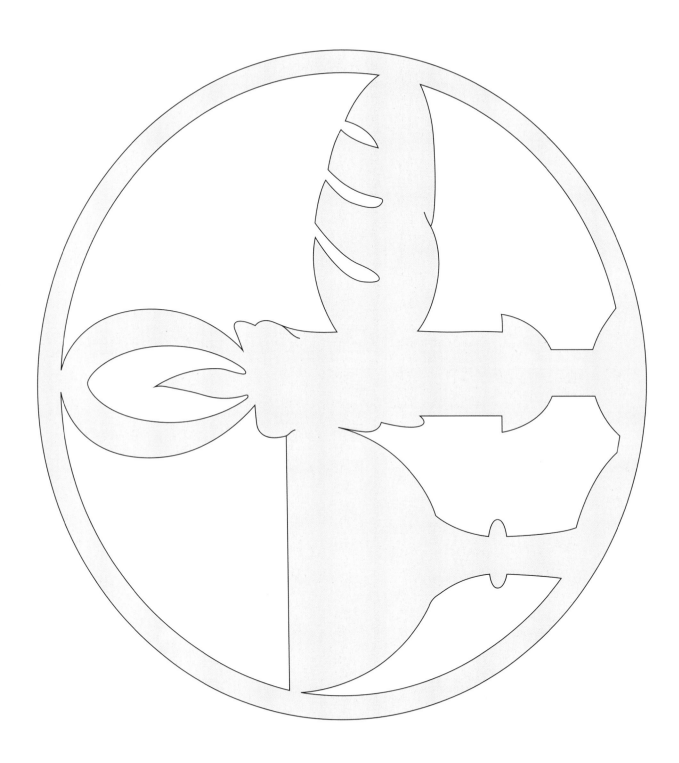

Communion with Candle

Bible

Dove

Fiery Dove

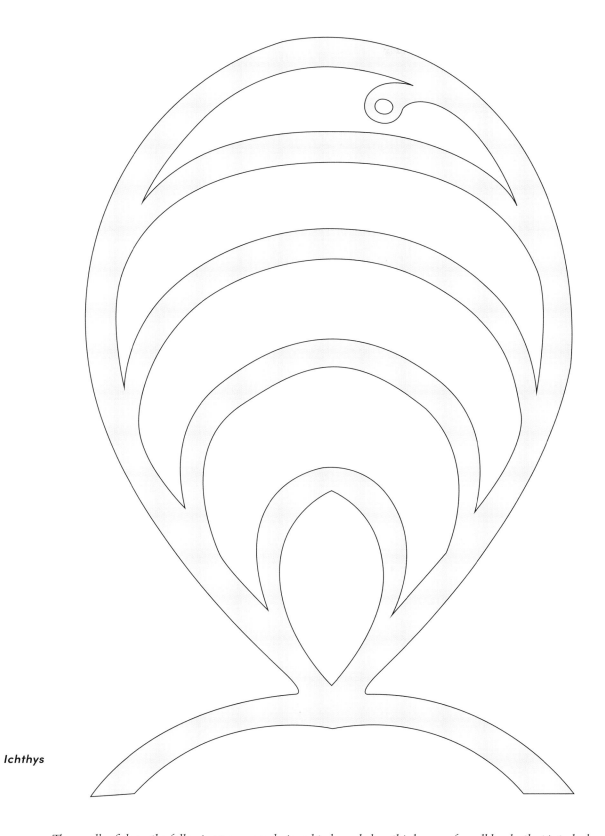

Ichthys

The smaller fish on the following pages are designed to hang below this by use of small hooks that interlock.

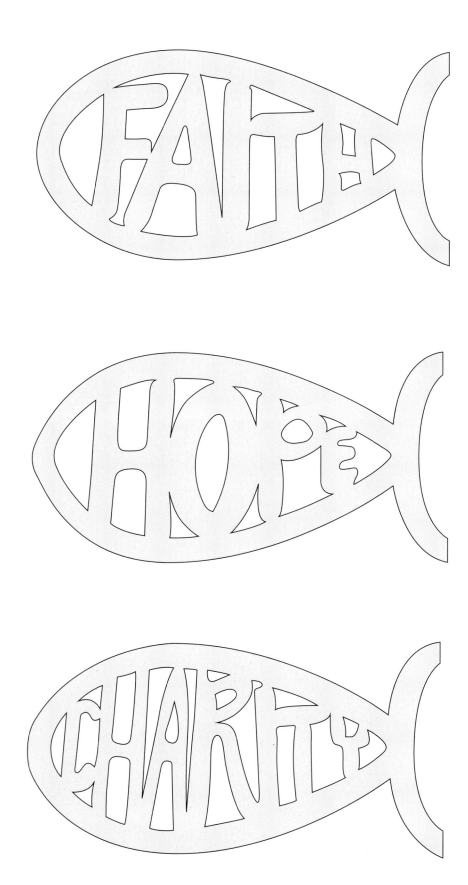

Jesus Praying

Jesus Walks with Children

Last Supper

Ascension

*Jonah and
the Whale*

Jesus in Prayer,
fretwork portrait, by Santomarco Enzo (Italy).

Photocopy at 130%

The Last Supper,
fretwork plaque, by Tom Zieg.

In His Arms,
segmentation plaque,
by Robin Balls.

Christmas Decorations and Ornaments

*Merry Christmas/
Noel Lettering*

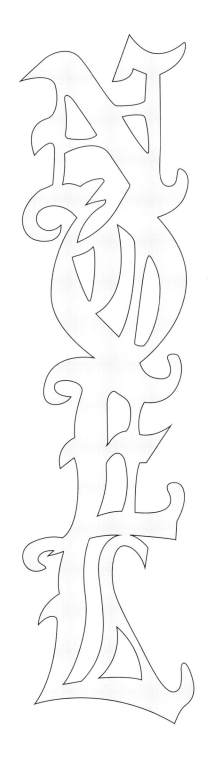

Christmas Tree Appliqué

Christmas Candle Appliqué

Simple Christmas Tree

Christmas Tree Ornament

**Ornate Christmas Tree
Ornament**

Christmas Candle Appliqué

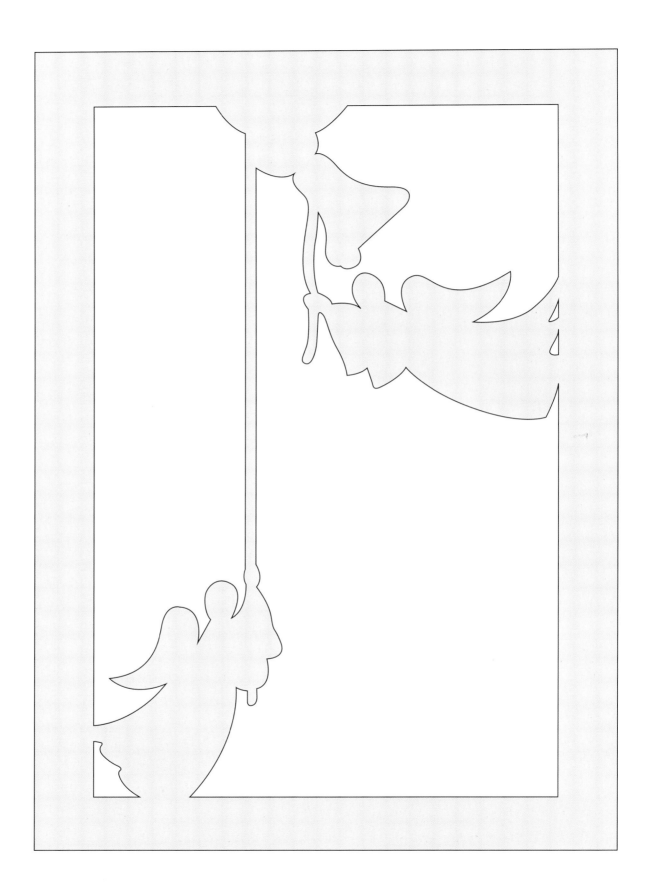

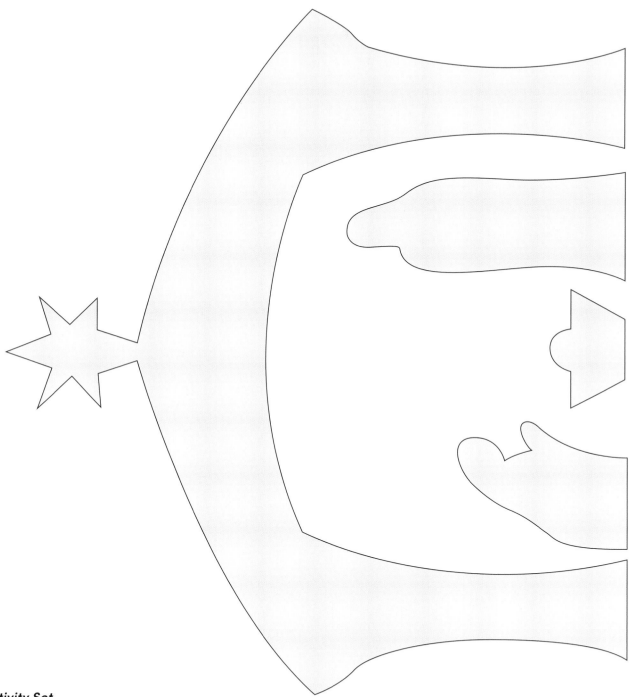

Nativity Set
This simple but classic Nativity scene contains 15 pieces found here on pages 105-109. Pieces can be left natural, stained, or painted. Gold leaf or paint can be used to accent the star.

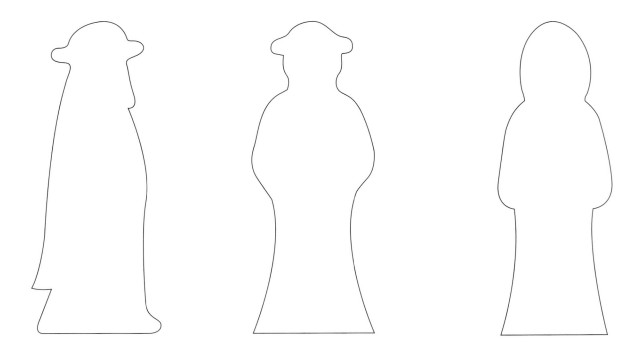

Shepherds

Three Wise Men and Camel

Angels and Bethlehem

Palm Trees

Joy Appliqué

Peace Appliqué

Fretwork Angel

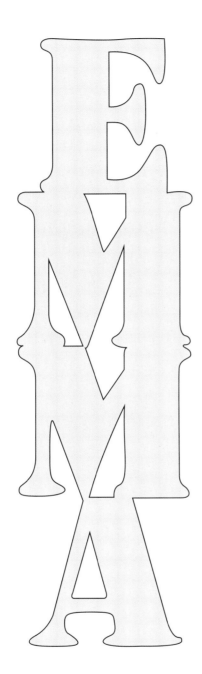
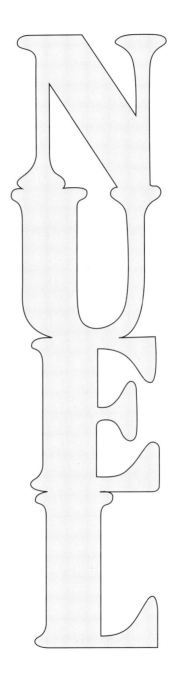

Emmanuel
Lettering

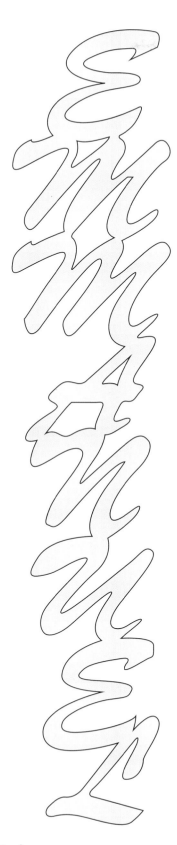

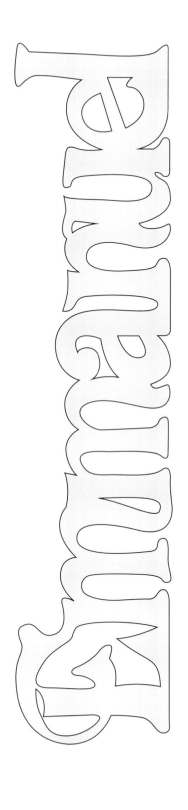

Emmanuel Lettering

Nativity Appliqué

Angel Trumpets

O Holy Night
This piece can be cut from solid wood,
plywood, or a platter blank.

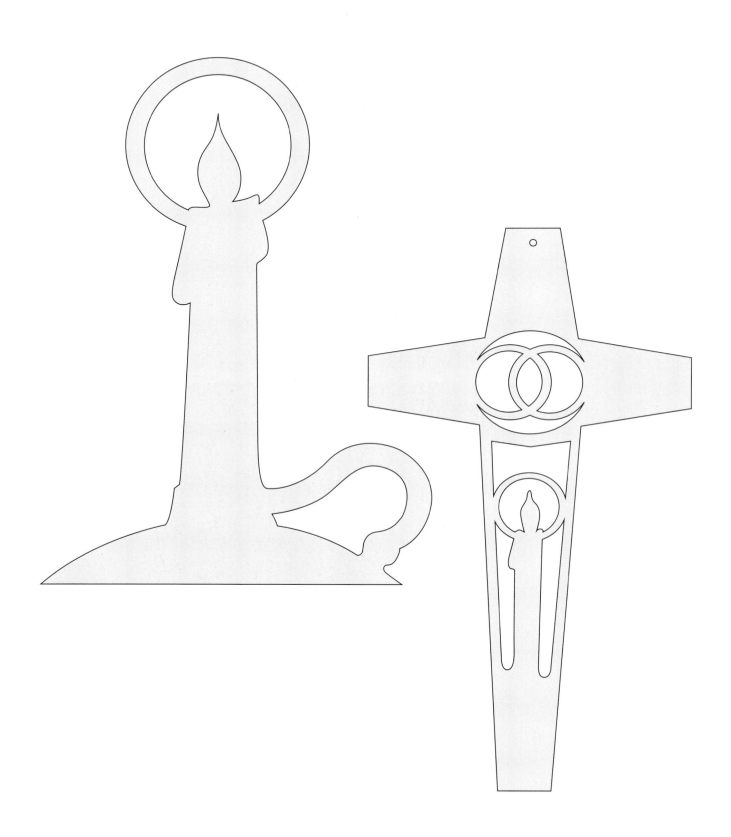

Guiding Light Candles

*Nativity
Ornament*

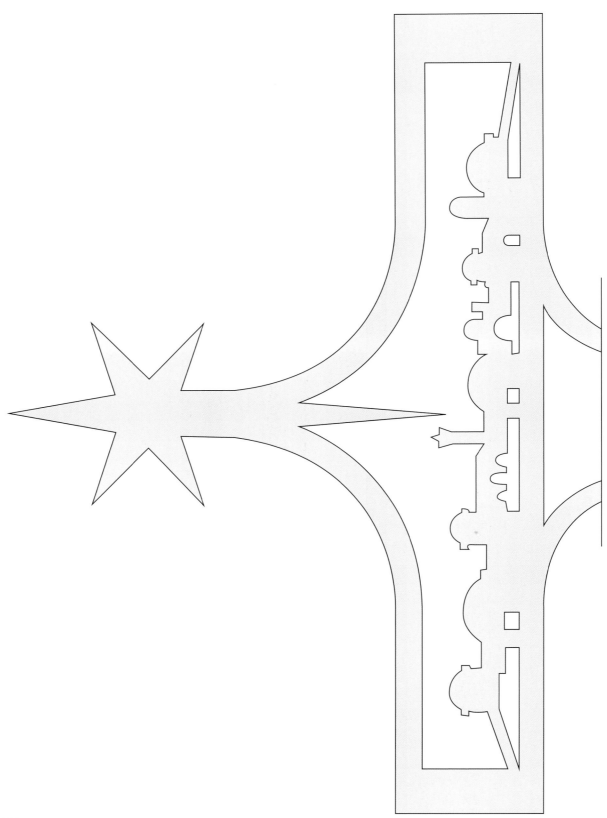

Bethlehem Scene

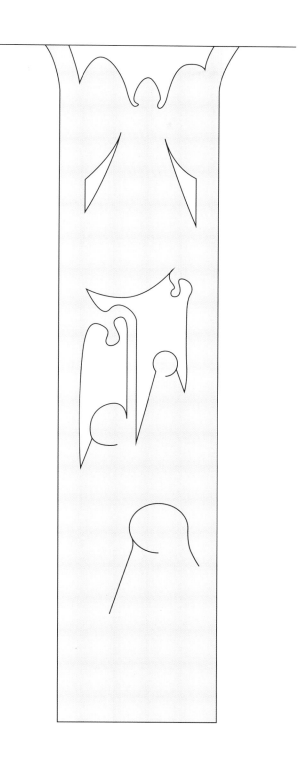

Anchor Cross

Mission Cross

Shepherd's Crook Cross

Bells

Nativity

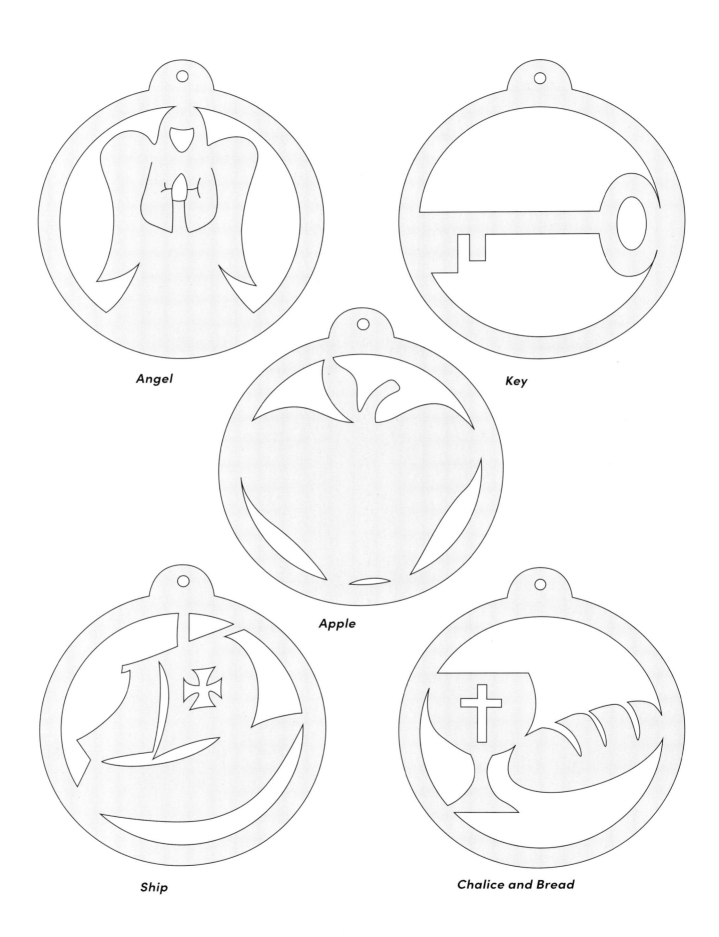

Angel

Key

Apple

Ship

Chalice and Bread

Palm Branch

Lily

Crown

Alpha and Omega

Star with Candle

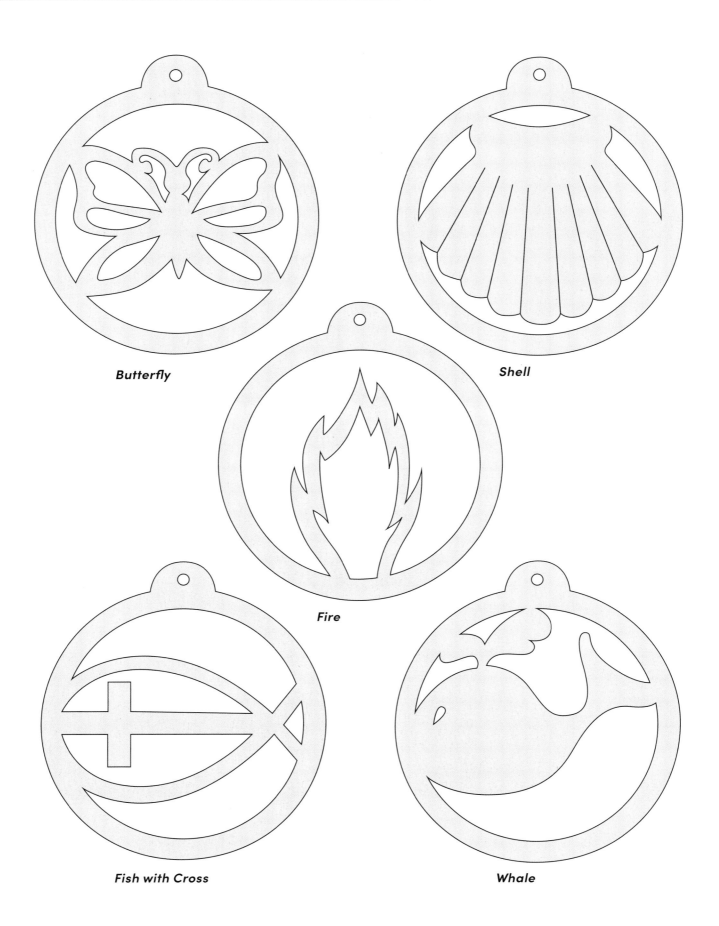

Butterfly

Shell

Fire

Fish with Cross

Whale

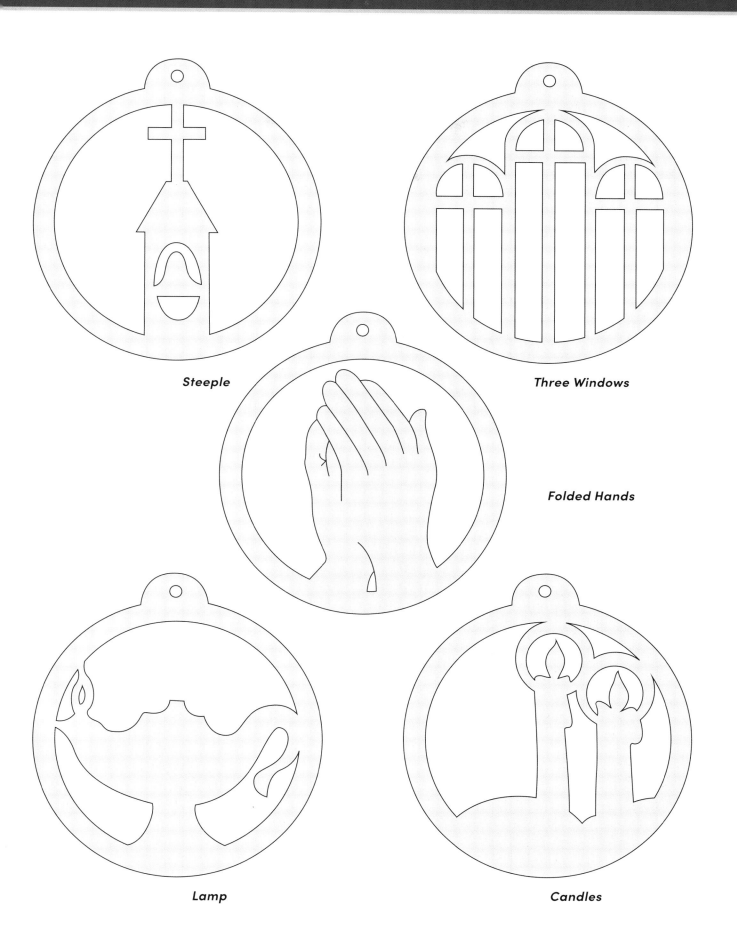

Steeple

Three Windows

Folded Hands

Lamp

Candles

Lantern

Star of the Apostles
Twelve-Point Star

Star

Christmas Tree

Cross Star
Four-Point Star

Bethlehem Star
Five-Point Star

Star of David
Six-Point Star

Mystic Star
Seven-Point Star

Star of Regeneration
Eight-Point Star

Fruits of the Spirit Star
Nine-Point Star

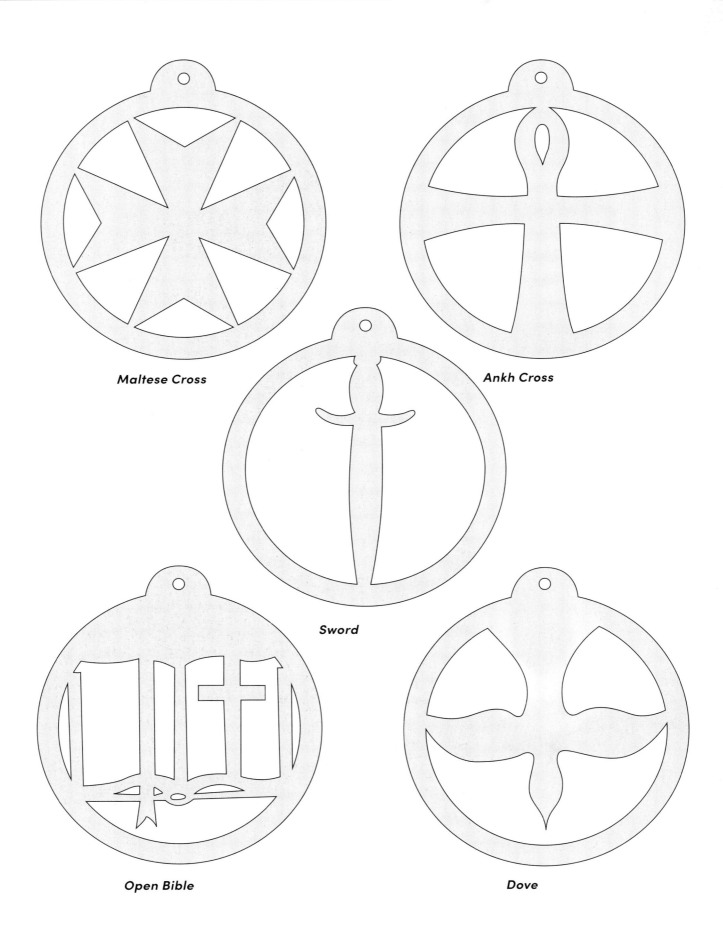

Maltese Cross

Ankh Cross

Sword

Open Bible

Dove

Water Droplets

Star of Bethlehem

Wise Men

Sunrise

Jesus Lives

Jesus Saves

Love

Tree

Three Crosses

Fleur-de-lis

Angel Trumpeting

Mary and Jesus

Angel

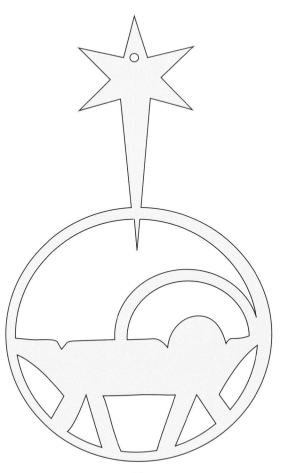

Manger

Star Ornament

Tree Ornament

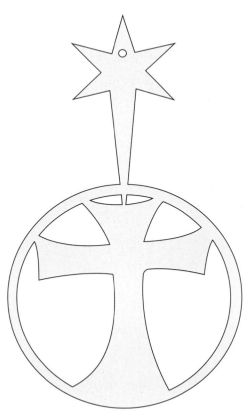

Cross Ornament

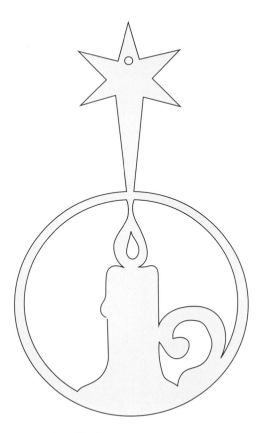

Candle Ornament

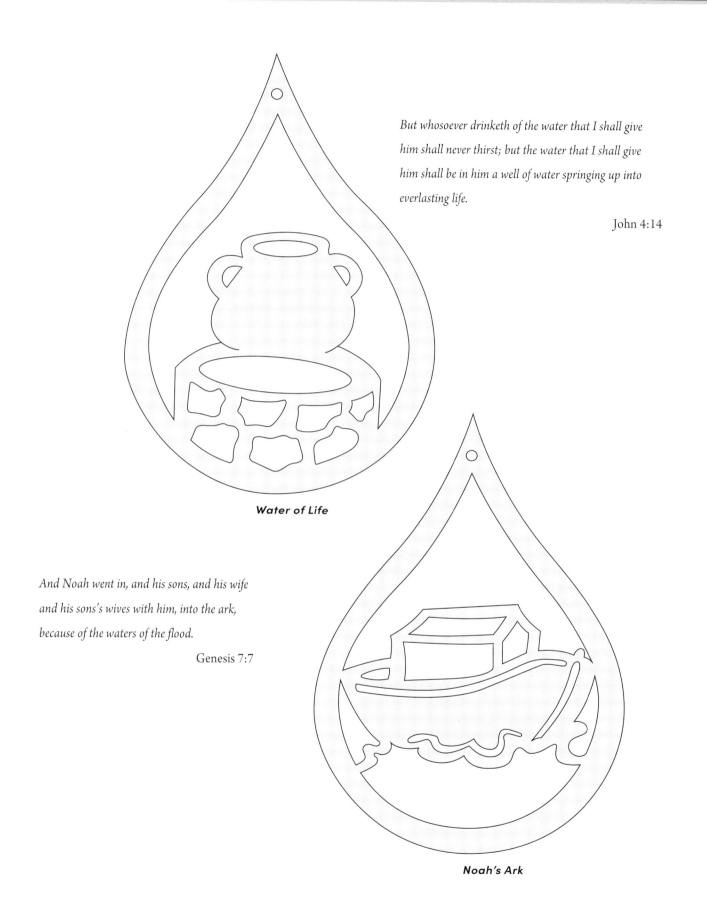

But whosoever drinketh of the water that I shall give him shall never thirst; but the water that I shall give him shall be in him a well of water springing up into everlasting life.

John 4:14

Water of Life

And Noah went in, and his sons, and his wife and his sons's wives with him, into the ark, because of the waters of the flood.

Genesis 7:7

Noah's Ark

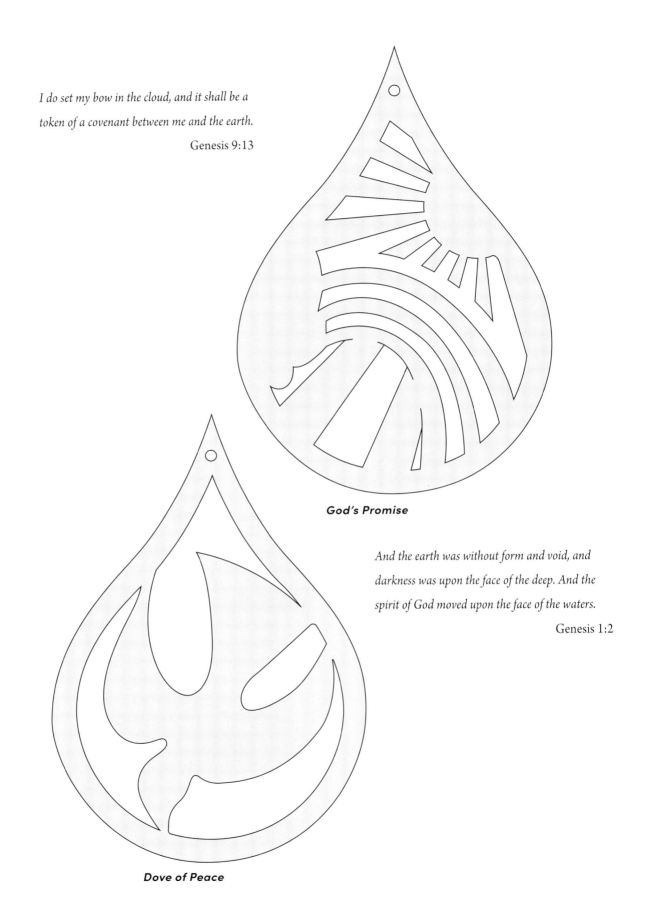

I do set my bow in the cloud, and it shall be a token of a covenant between me and the earth.

Genesis 9:13

God's Promise

And the earth was without form and void, and darkness was upon the face of the deep. And the spirit of God moved upon the face of the waters.

Genesis 1:2

Dove of Peace

Which hope we have as an anchor of the soul, both sure and steadfast, and which entereth into the veil.

Hebrews 6:19

Anchor of Hope

He will swallow up death in victory; and the Lord God will wipe away tears from all faces.

Isaiah 25:8

Victory Cross

*And straightaway they forsook their nets, and
followed him.*

Mark 1:18

Fisher of Men

*John answered, saying unto them all, I indeed
baptize you with water; but one mightier
than I cometh, the latchet of whose shoes I am
worthy to unloose: he shall baptize you with
the Holy Ghost and with fire.*

Luke 3:16

Fire of the Spirit

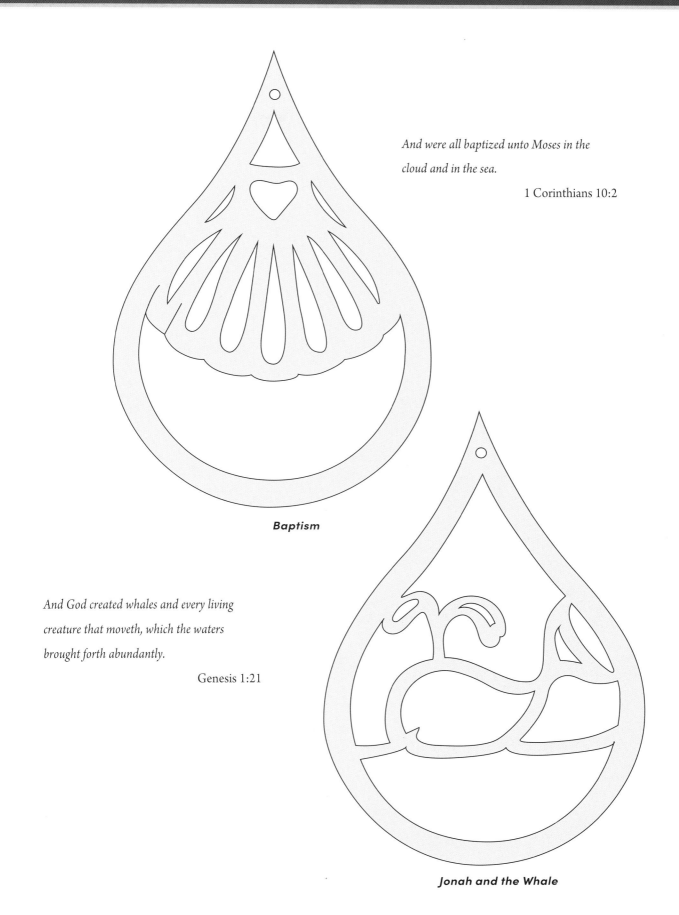

And were all baptized unto Moses in the cloud and in the sea.

1 Corinthians 10:2

Baptism

And God created whales and every living creature that moveth, which the waters brought forth abundantly.

Genesis 1:21

Jonah and the Whale

Various Cross Ornaments

Joy/Noel Ornaments

Trinity Ornament

Cross
Ornaments

Chi Rho
Ornaments

Trinity Ornament

Christmas Greetings,
fretwork ornaments,
by Jeff Paxton.

Peace Angel
Fretwork pattern by Carol Behrer.

Photocopy at 125%

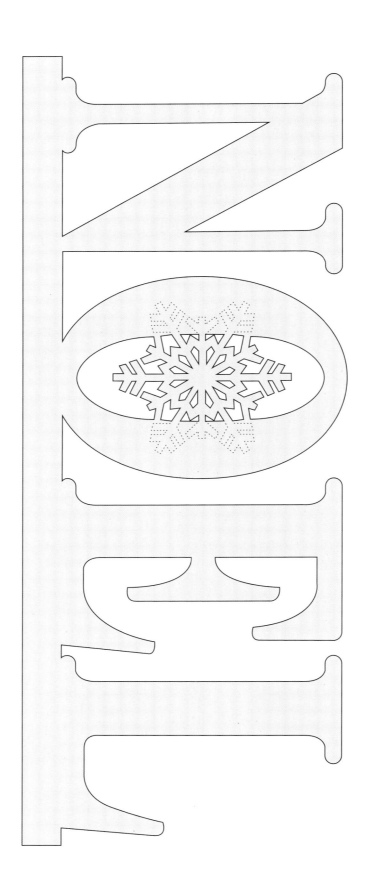

The First Noel
Word art by Bruce Shea.

Photocopy at 125%

Use these lines as reference when drilling hole

O Holy Night
Word art pattern by Bruce Shea.

Photocopy at 150%

Christmas Arch
Patterns by Beatrix Brockman.

Photocopy at 250%

Christmas Arch
Patterns by Beatrix Brockman.

Photocopy at 250%

Christmas Arch
Patterns by Beatrix Brockman.

Photocopy at 250%

Filigree Star Ornaments
Fretwork patterns by Keith Fenton.

Photocopy at 125%

Holiday Ribbon Mini Plaques
Fretwork patterns by Sheila Landry.

Photocopy at 125%

Jigsaw Puzzle Ornaments

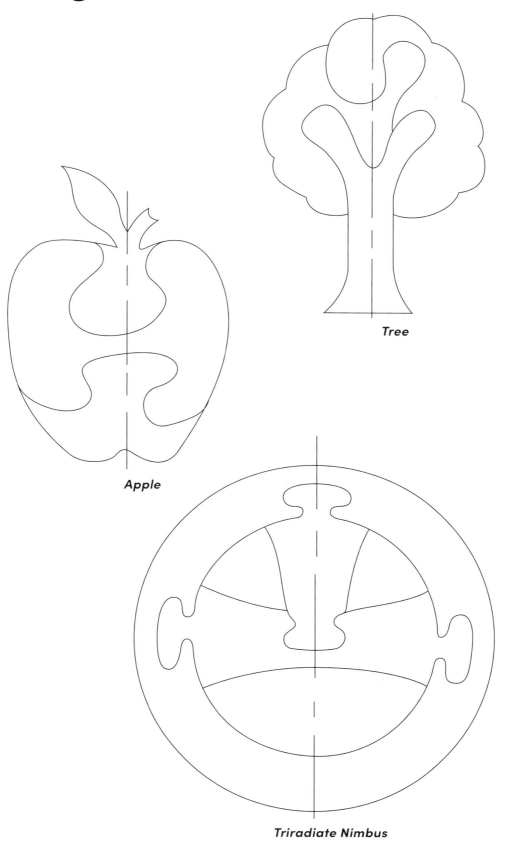

Tree

Apple

Triradiate Nimbus

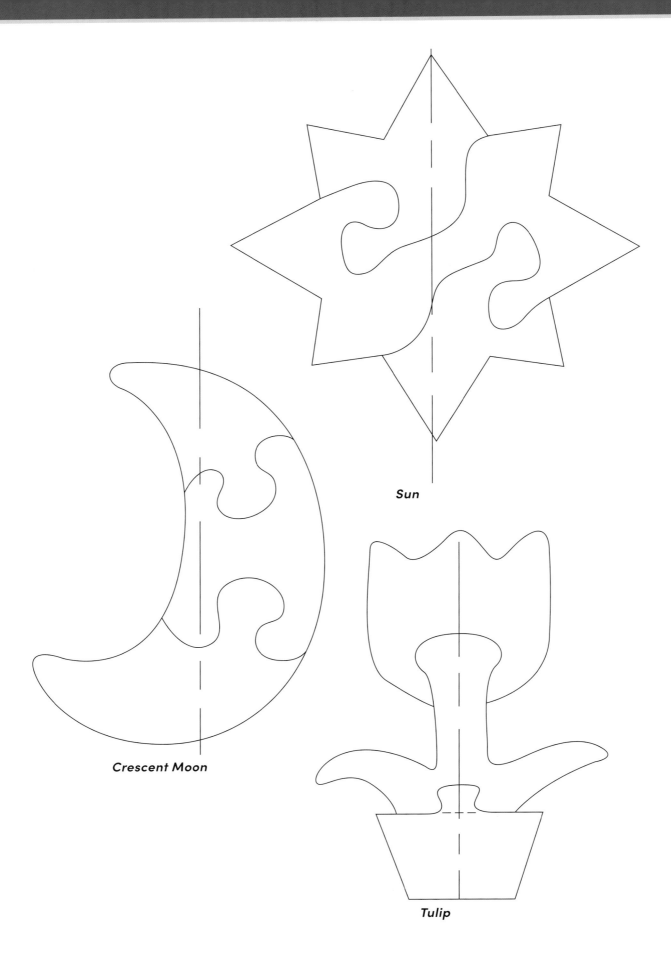

Sun

Crescent Moon

Tulip

Angel

Angel

Angel

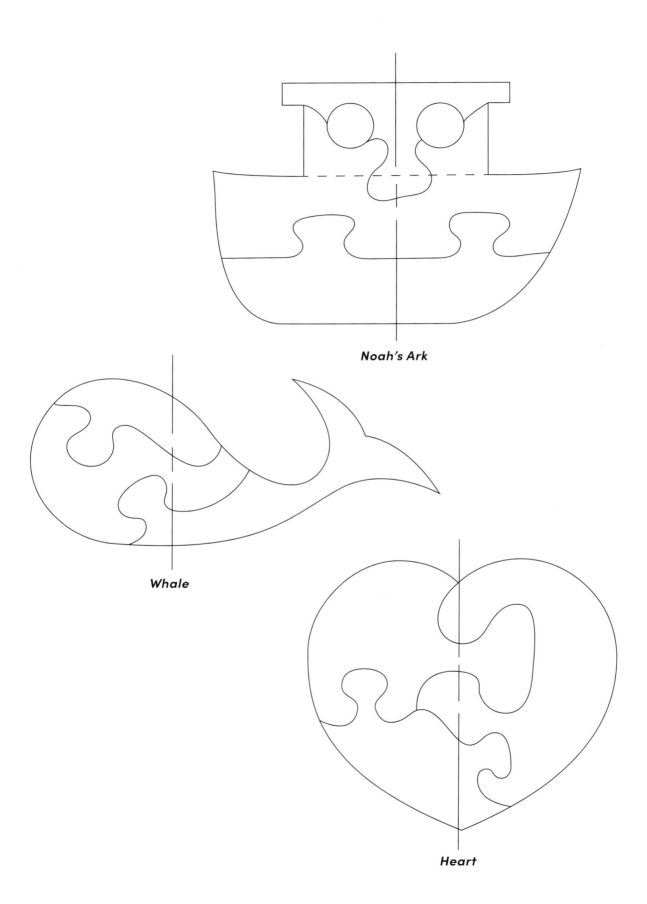

Noah's Ark

Whale

Heart

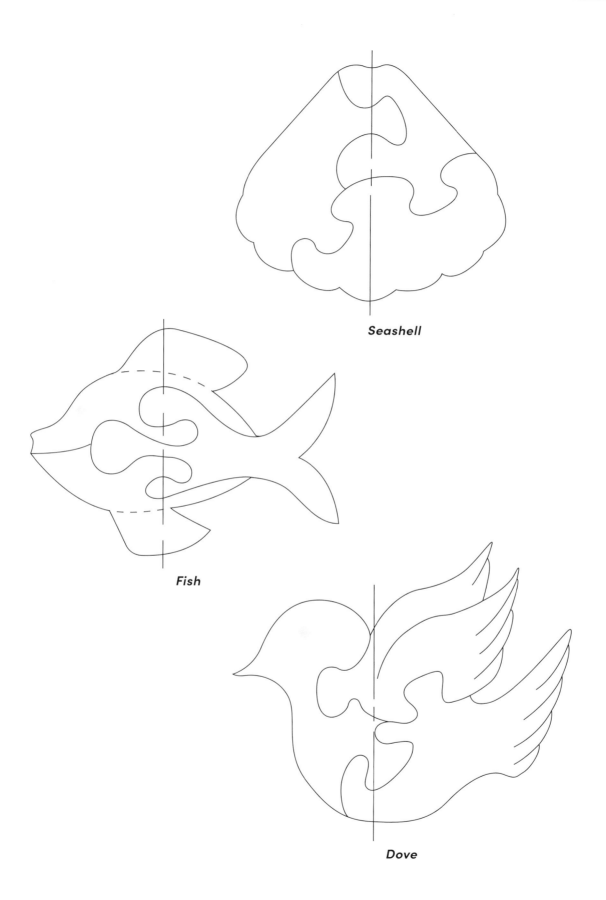

Seashell

Fish

Dove

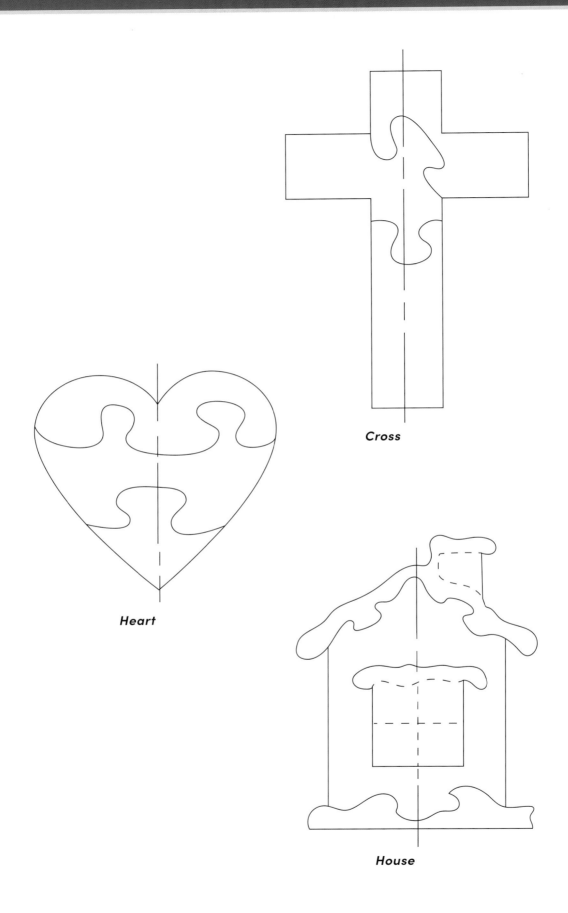

Cross

Heart

House

Star

Wreath

Bell

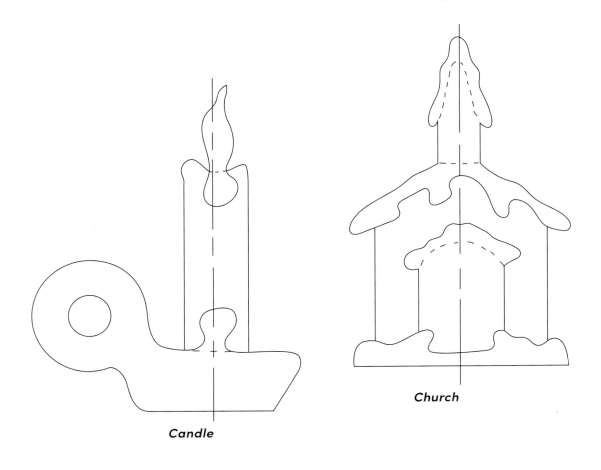

Candle

Church

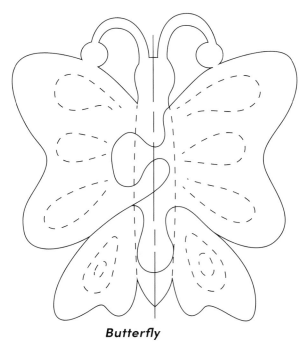

Butterfly

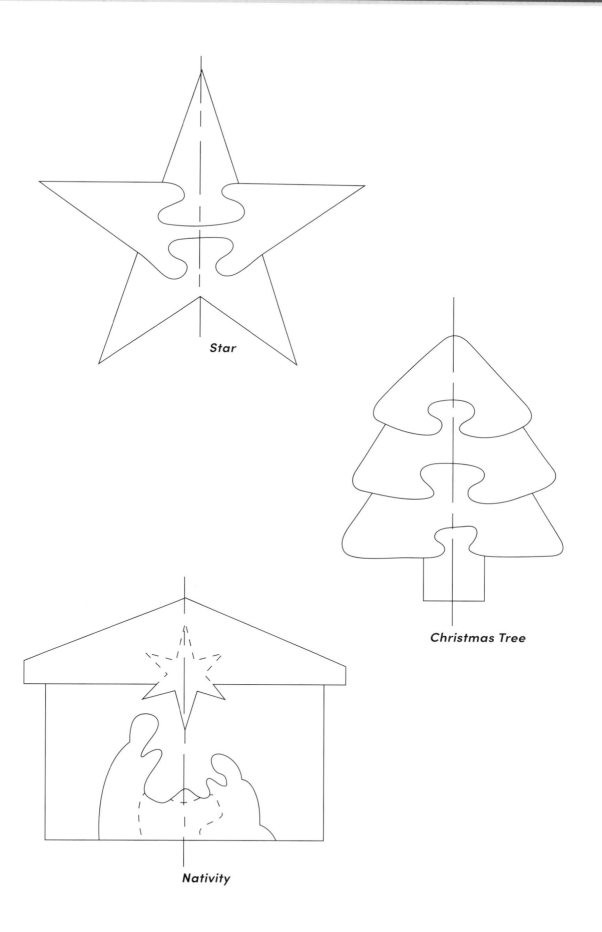

Star

Christmas Tree

Nativity

Letter Openers

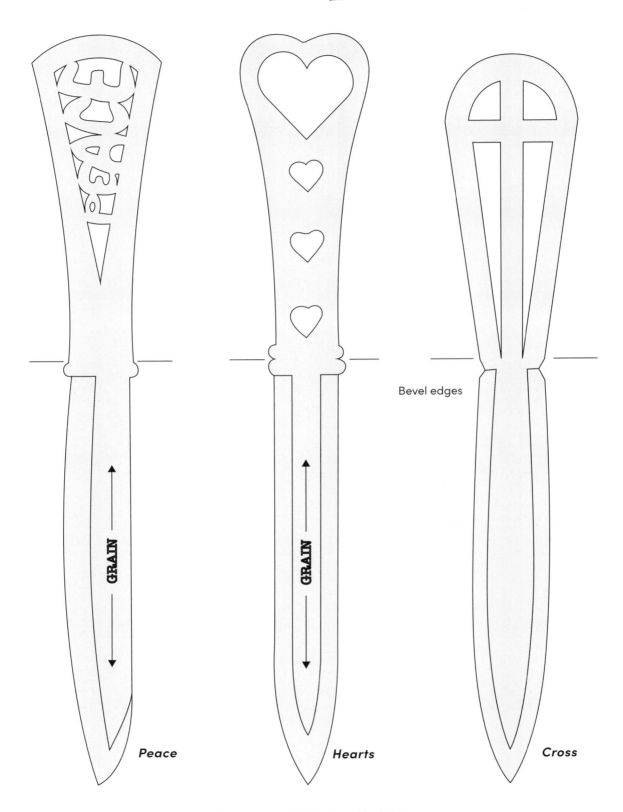

Bevel edges

GRAIN

GRAIN

Peace

Hearts

Cross

Note: Solid hardwood should be used for the letter openers

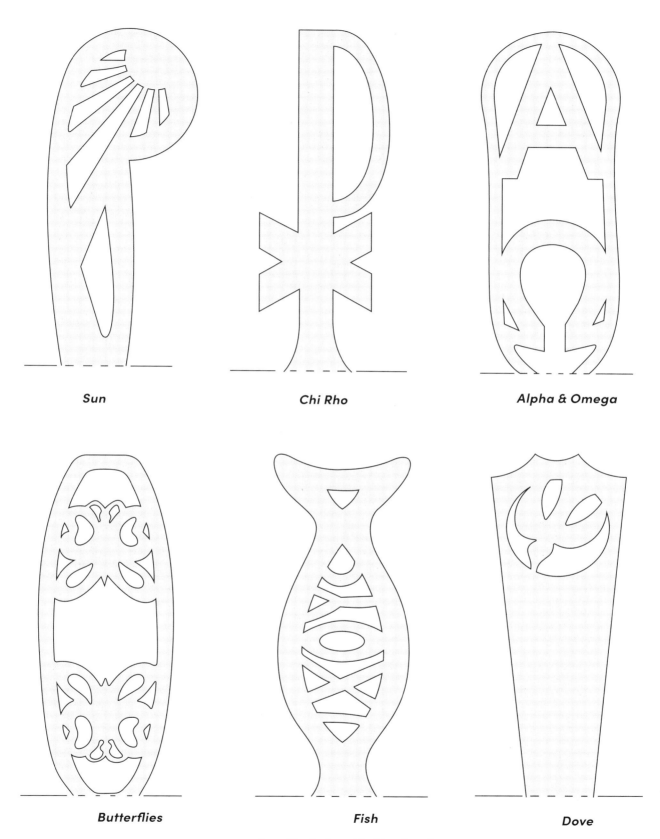

Sun

Chi Rho

Alpha & Omega

Butterflies

Fish

Dove

Ixoyc: The Greek word for fish. It formed an acrostic of the Greek phrase "Jesus Christ, God's Son."

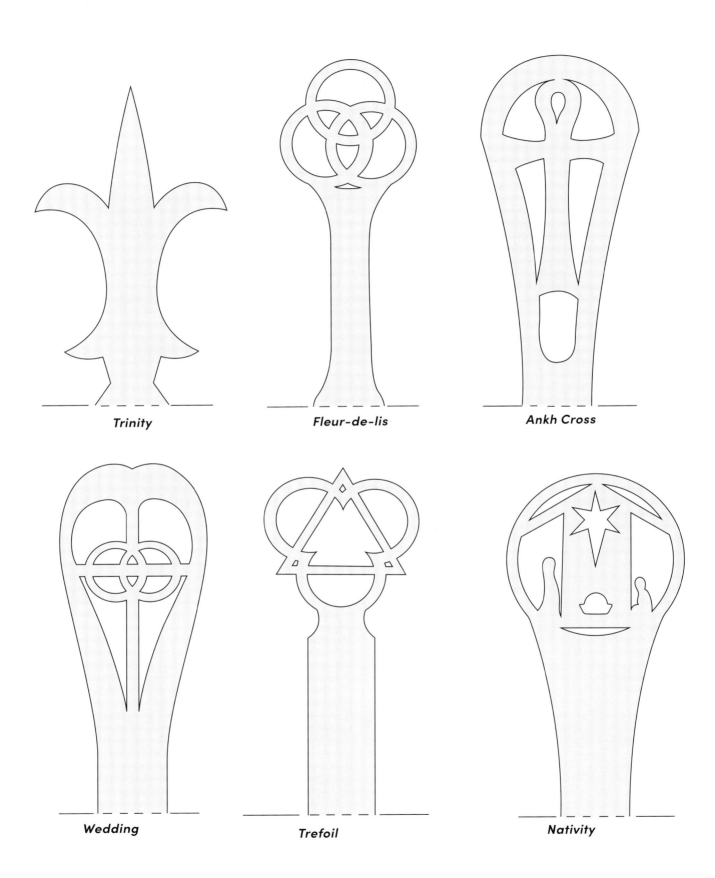

Trinity

Fleur-de-lis

Ankh Cross

Wedding

Trefoil

Nativity

Children's Three-Dimensional Cutout Projects

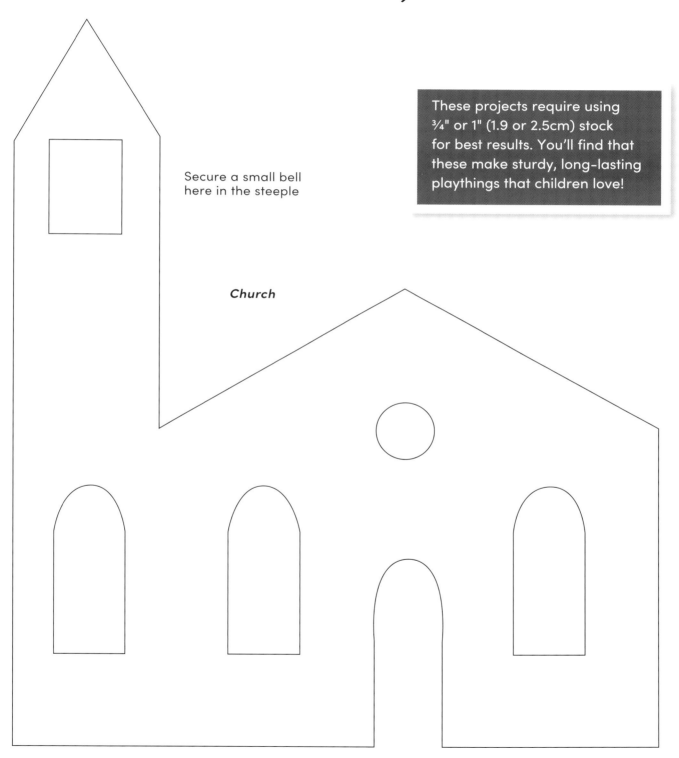

Secure a small bell here in the steeple

These projects require using ¾" or 1" (1.9 or 2.5cm) stock for best results. You'll find that these make sturdy, long-lasting playthings that children love!

Church

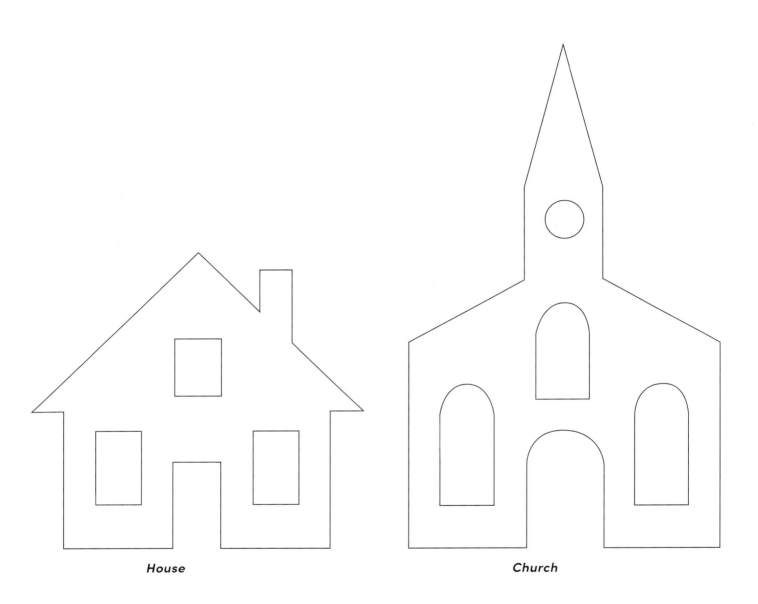

House

Church

Tree

Church

Open Bible

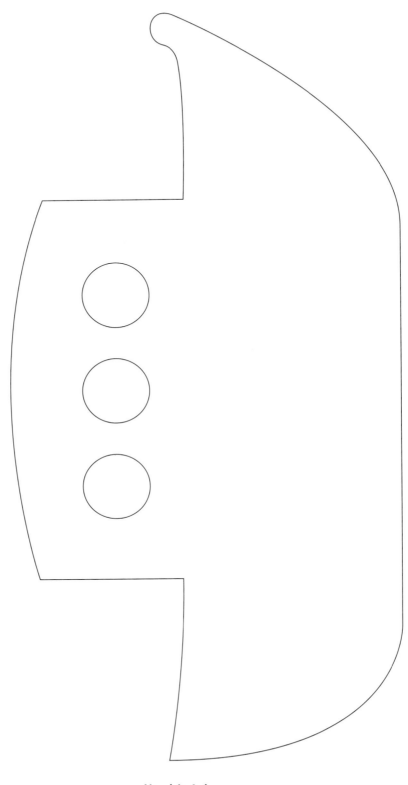

Noah's Ark

Dove

Hippopotamus

Sheep

Pig

Giraffe

Camel

Rainbow/Clouds/Sun

Horse

Elephant

Cow

These are popular projects for a child's room. Drill a hole in top for use as candle holders. With the addition of a simple rectangular base, they also make a nice set of bookends.

Children Praying

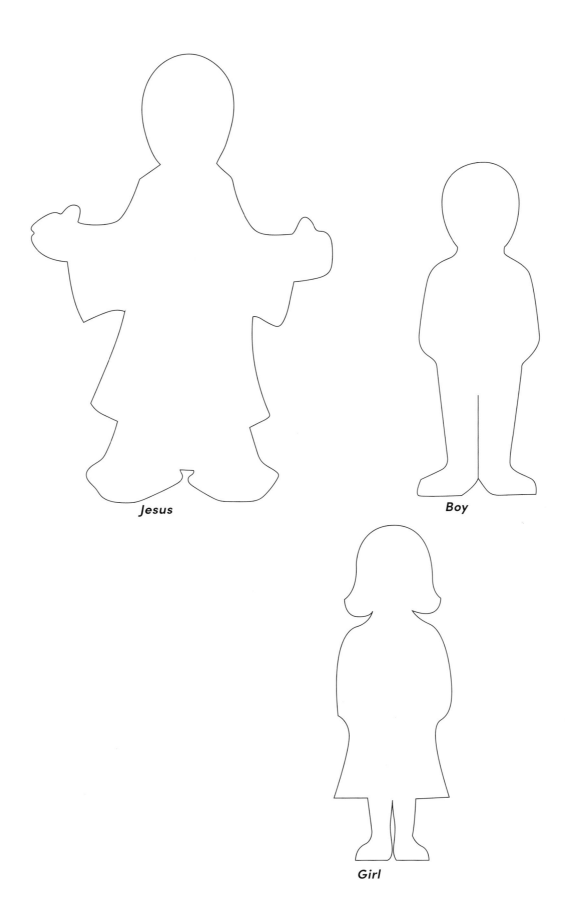

Jesus

Boy

Girl

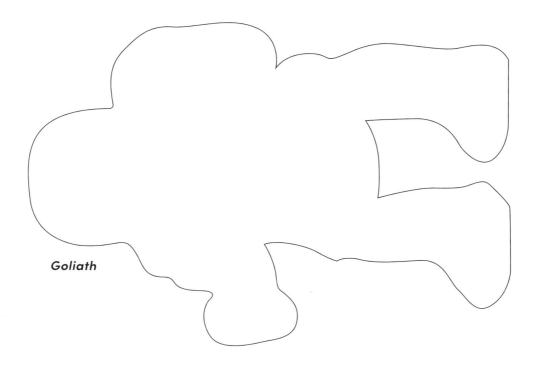

Goliath

Drill hole prior to cutting out spearhead shape.

Wood dowel for spear handle

Drill hole for dowel in hand and spearhead. Glue dowel into each part.

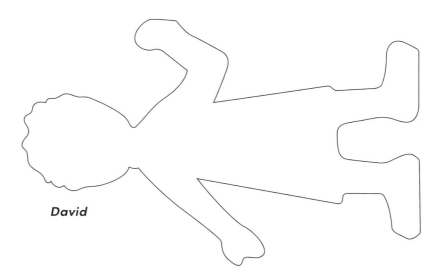

David

Tree with Serpent

Adam

Eve

Daniel and the Lions

Jonah and the Whale

Puzzles

Note: Puzzle patterns should be enlarged by at least 165%.

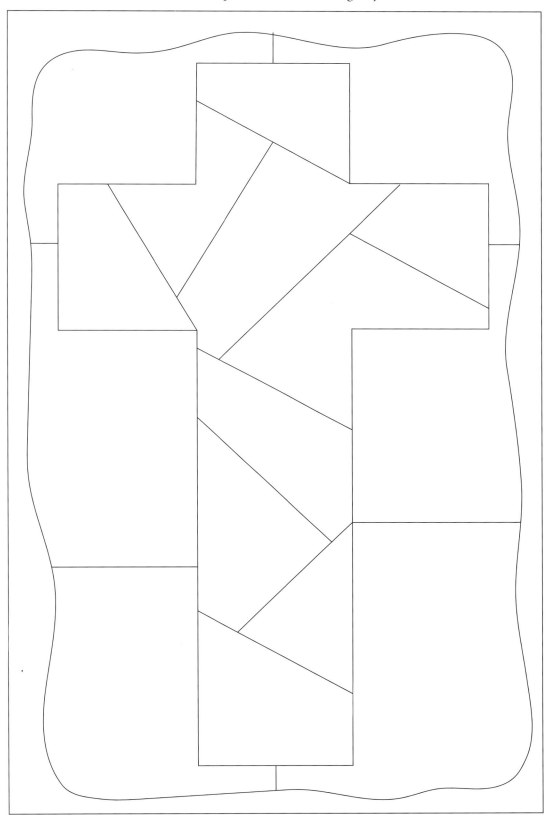

Cross

Noah's Ark—Genesis,
Chapters 6-8

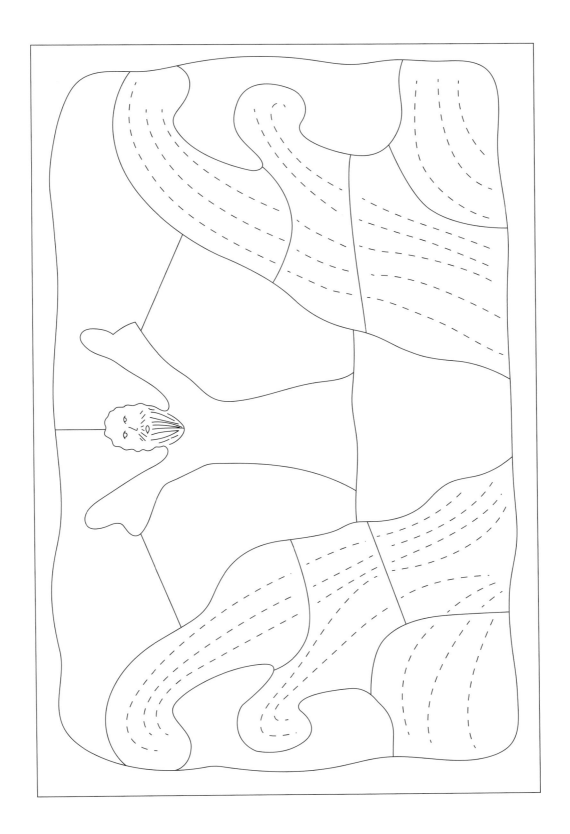

Moses Parting the Red Sea—Exodus, Chapter 14

Daniel in the Lion's Den—
Daniel, Chapter 6

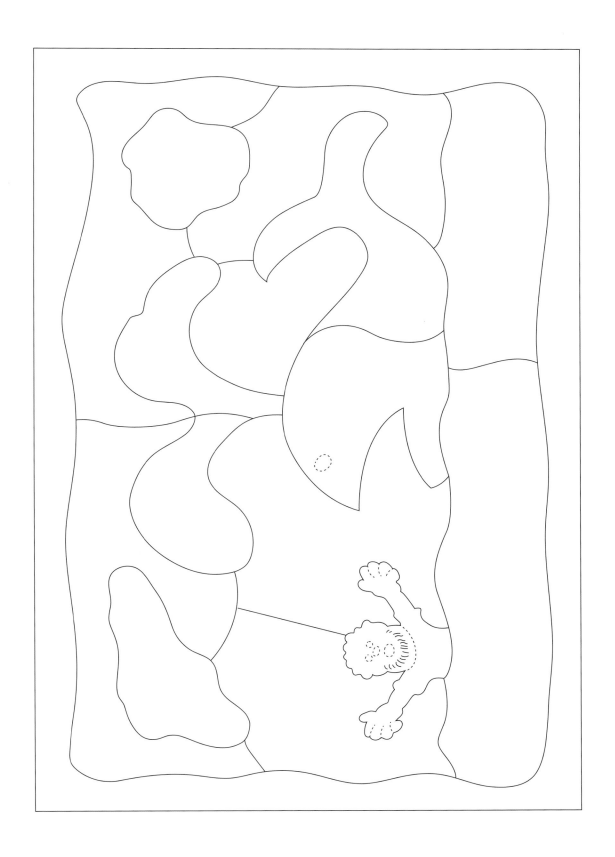

Jonah and the Whale—
Jonah, Chapters 1–2

Jesus is Born—
Luke, Chapter 2

Christ Has Risen—
John, Chapters 18-20

Letters and Words

IHC or IHS
The first three letters of Jesus in Greek. Some Greek letters have several forms in English.

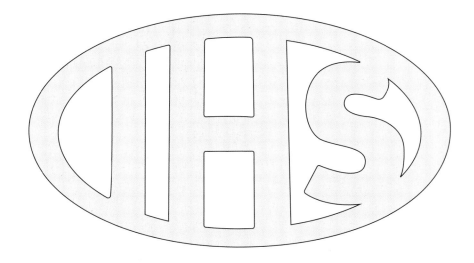

INRI
The first letters of the words in the Latin superscription, "Jesus Nazarenus Rex Iudaeorum" (Jesus of Nazareth, King of the Jews.) The superscription was on the upper part of the cross on which Jesus was crucified.

NIKA
The Greek word for conquer, conqueror, or victor.

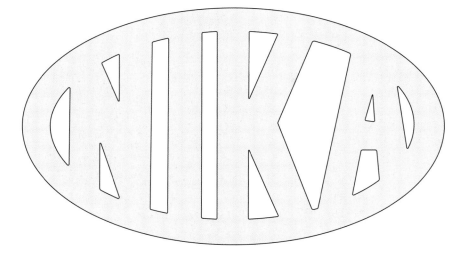

ALPHA OMEGA

Alpha and Omega have been added to emblems to symbolize the divinity of Christ since the fourth century. They are the first and last letters, representing the beginning and the end. (See Revelation 22:13.)

Chi Rho

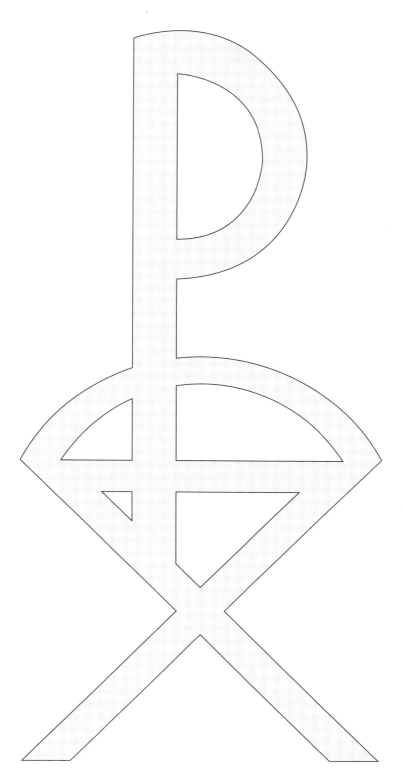

Chi Rho
Combined in a symbolic
representation of Christ's birth.

Numbers

God Loves You Cross

Anchor Cross
An early Christian symbol of hope. This cross is from the days of Christian persecution. Christians saw hope in the anchor, while non-Christians only saw the anchor.

Marriage Cross
The two rings in this design symbolize the unity of two parties. The cross, with the dove flying down, represents connectedness to God.

Resurrection Cross
This design features the crosses at Golgotha and features vines and butterflies, both symbols of renewal and resurrection.

Heart of Faith Cross
A minimalist cross with a central heart, embodying the core truth of Christianity—that at the heart of faith lies love, a love that's both received from and given to the divine.